DISPLACED PERSONS

Theological Reflection on Immigration, Refugees, and Marginalization

Matthew W. Charlton
and Timothy S. Moore
General Editors

D1548069

Displaced Persons: Theological Reflection on Immigration, Refugees, and Marginalization

The General Board of Higher Education and Ministry leads and serves The United Methodist Church in the recruitment, preparation, nurture, education, and support of Christian leaders—lay and clergy—for the work of making disciples of Jesus Christ for the transformation of the world. Its vision is that a new generation of Christian leaders will commit boldly to Jesus Christ and be characterized by intellectual excellence, moral integrity, spiritual courage, and holiness of heart and life. The General Board of Higher Education and Ministry of The United Methodist Church serves as an advocate for the intellectual life of the church. The Board's mission embodies the Wesleyan tradition of commitment to the education of laypersons and ordained persons by providing access to higher education for all persons.

HIGHER EDUCATION & MINISTRY
General Board of Higher Education and Ministry
THE UNITED METHODIST CHURCH

To the children, women, and men who dare the peril of the seas, the heat of the desert, and the backlash against their humanity. May they find home and peace in a compassionate land, surrounded by those who know them to be beloved children of God.

CONTENTS

INTRODUCTION
The Displaced Person

Timothy S. Moore

"Italy and France Call for More Integrated EU Action on Migrants"

"Fury over Refugee Ban"

"Britain Is Becoming More Fenced Off, Vindictive and Callous: The Hard Truth about Refugees"

"Undocumented Immigrants Are Facing Deportation"

"Homeland Security Unveils Sweeping Plan to Deport"

"4.5 Million Refugees from Syria's Civil War"

"1 Million Children Refugees from South Sudan's Civil War"

These statements are headlines. Taken from various newspapers, these headlines represent only a narrow sample. This cursory survey of headlines offers a stark image of our global community's heaving and fluid social matrix. Political refugees flee persecution. Economic migrants seek a better life. Children and their families scramble to evade war. Immigrants experience hostility. Communities labor to cope with new realties, straining and stretching assumptions about what defines and sustains the social fabric. These headlines describe a sweeping and complex phenomenon of displacement.

Yet the issue of displacement is more than sweeping and complex. In many ways, these headlines about displacement do not offer just a flat image but act as an icon, granting a glimpse through them to something far more profound, to pervasive circumstances and systems defining what it means to live in today's world. Moreover, these circumstances and systems do not represent abstract debates about good public policy or proper civic or ecclesial responses. Rather, these circumstances and systems represent the flesh-and-blood realities of our lives and the lives of those we know, the communities in which we live, and the societies we seek to press toward being more perfect unions. Whether consciously or not, our individual lives, our personal networks, our churches and ministries and families and campuses are all directly affected by the social and intellectual recalibrations eventuated by such persisting and inescapable displacement.

In particular our campuses represent a unique nexus. Often perceived as ivory towers detached from the mundanity of real life, the truth of the matter is rather the inverse. Campuses are places where the world mixes. In real time, this mixing presents a conceptual and practical struggle to integrate and address many of the issues that for others are merely read as headlines or as scrolling banners on the bottom of a webpage. Campuses are a microcosmic expression of that global convolution. As it turns out, the displacement that we see writ boldly across the top fold of our newsprint is more than a description of migration, immigration, and social and political reconstructions. Those displacements describe an experienced account for only a portion of the change and uncertainly defining our existence.

When families and individuals displace—either forcibly or voluntarily—assumptions about the world shift. Concrete certainties confront alternative convictions. Social positions are challenged and changed. Meaning slips. New assumptions coalesce. Questions replace answers. Possibilities present while other opportunities recede. Our college and university campuses serve as cultural gravitational epicenters, attracting these challenging world issues and often convulsive personal experiences to the same place. Such places necessitate nimble and creative thinkers to help lead those campus communities to address these displacements in authentic and meaningful ways. Fortunately, necessity affords opportunity.

Campus leaders have the rich opportunity to shape conversations and to provide support and direction that nurture new faith communities and cultivate transformative and authentic responses. The formation of new communities populated by students and other campus leaders capable of providing the kind of transformative response required is difficult to achieve alone.

In imagining this yawning range of displacement manifest on the campus and the expansive skills needed by campus leaders to help facilitate faithful and effective change, we conceived of a volume written by the campus, for the campus. With contributors coming from many perspectives and ministerial settings and countries, all contributors share common commitments to this vital work on the campus as a locus for social change and spiritual renewal while laboring to speak faithfully and robustly to very particular contexts, addressing very specific concerns.

The title for the volume—*Displaced Persons*—borrows from a similarly titled short story by Flannery O'Connor written in the middle part of the last century. In a practical way, O'Connor's short story not only supplies the name for this collection of essays but also provides the intellectual frame within which the substance of these authors' contributions is arranged. Her narrative captures the complex striations a single displacement actually represents.

O'Connor's short story tells the tale of an immigrant family's—the Guizacs'—displacement from post–World War II Poland and their relocation to a small southern town in 1950s America. Ostensibly, the story is about political refugees. But, like most dislocations, that one change impacts in unexpected ways and exposes other, underlying issues and displacements. Quickly, issues of religion, class, race, and culture are all exposed and confronted by this single event. Some in her story leave voluntarily. Some are threatened with removal. Death invades. And, all the while, latent dehumanization of the other provides a binding thread to weave the whole story into a blanketing pall laying heavily upon the narrative's landscape.

Determinedly international in perspective, our volume attempts to wander assiduously over this same imaginative landscape, pausing to focus on specific issues of displacement exposed when attended to deliberately. Some contributors consider the particular displacements of young adults within the life of the church, pondering the specific impact such displacements have upon young adults and the larger body from which they are dislocated. Taking up a similar line of questioning, another writer assesses a distinct population of young adults—Native American college students—and their search for place and belonging in a denomination ambiguously receptive to young people, generally, and young people from a marginal community all the more. One essayist focuses on how communities on our campuses find themselves marginalized and how collegiate ministries might function to re-integrate and repair or to generate and exacerbate dislocation. Yet, another contributor pauses to contemplate mediation, especially mediation needed in a world increasingly defined by liminality. Writing from his perspective as a minister serving in a United Methodist congregation in Germany, his ef-forts attend to the church's potential role in such a place, negotiating rela-tionships and community between migrant and native populations, younger and older generations.

One author examines what it means to experience an internal, personal dislocation, lingering to consider the consequences of a disembodied sexual ethic. Other writers attend to the place of faith on the college or university campus, one focusing on the potential overlap between the hermeneuti-cal strategies of the Wesleyan Quadrilateral and Islamic jurisprudence with another considering the efficacious role a collegiate ministry might serve as a practical expression of the incarnation and manifestation of the beloved kingdom within the academy. Still others write from the perspective of leaders and ministers in communities where displacement means absence, considering what it means to cope and care in a society where some whole families have migrated elsewhere and other families have been severed by migration's exigencies. A final chapter attempts to frame the whole global refugee crisis within the matrix of home, using theologically poignant ques-tions to shape our considerations and provoke our responses.

As in O'Connor's story, seeing one displacement supplies the opportunity to find many more. Sometimes related yet always present, displacements on our campuses and in our communities require concerted and deliberate efforts to see them correctly, to find any correlating dislocations otherwise unnoticed, to name unrelated dislocations that might be similarly present, and to imagine ways to speak honestly and forthrightly about them all, if they are to be addressed and remedied in authentic and faithful ways.

Prominently featured throughout O'Connor's story are the itinerant meanderings of a peacock. The peacock's presence is a useful foil for O'Connor as a serviceable yet subtle interjection of Christ into her narrative. Long associated with Christ, the peacock symbolizes a divine omnipresence that is visceral, common, distant, and distinct yet accessible and known. However, for O'Connor, the peacock suggests more than divine presence; it suggests divine vigilance. Near the beginning of her short story, O'Connor's peacock is seen pausing in the yard, staring "fixed in the distance on something no one else [can] see." Here, O'Connor's Christ is both present yet able to penetrate beyond what is patent and observe what others might have overlooked, ignored, or been unable to see. If this volume does anything, we hope it offers the peacock's perspective on our world, our campuses, and the church. In a world blighted by children fleeing war, buoyed by some seeking a better, more hopeful life, and scarred by the fabric of family rent by those advocating "zero tolerance," it is our prayer that this perspective comes with a lingering moment of pause, allowing this volume's writers and those who read it the occasion and tools to see what we, too, might otherwise have failed to see.

THE UPROOTED PLANT
AND THE SACRAMENTS

Matt Barlow

Missionary Pastor, English-Language Ministries in Cottbus,
United Methodist Church

Introduction

how easy it is to kill the uprooted plant, especially when you put it down in hostile soil."[1] This quotation, one of many insightful ones from Frank Herbert's seminal work, *Dune*, encapsulates the challenges facing young migrants in a German context today. In many cases the soil is hostile with migrants being attacked, refugee shelters being burned, and a heightened political rhetoric that plays into racial stereotypes and xenophobia—rhetoric that is not the sole domain of fringe parties. As recently as September 2015, the Interior Minister of Bavaria Joachim Herrmann, who belongs to the CSU—a party in the current ruling coalition—made the statement on national television, "Roberto Blanco [a popular singer] war immer ein wunderbarer Neger"[2] (Roberto Blanco was always a wonderful nigger). Hostile soil indeed.

---

1 Frank Herbert, *Dune* (London: Hodder & Stoughton, 2005), 79.

2 "Neger"-Äußerung von Bayerns Innenminister: "Ich verwende das Wort sonst überhaupt nicht," *Der Spiegel*, 1 September 2015, accessed 27 April 2016, http://www.spiegel.de/politik/deutschland

If the soil in Germany is not hostile then it is often merely apathetic. However, staying within Frank Herbert's metaphor, a plant can just as easily die from apathy as from hostility. This is not to paint an entirely negative image of Germany. If it comes across that way then it is simply because, for a migrant, it is currently quite difficult to escape the negative aspects of German views on migrants. I sometimes wonder if it is possible for a migrant not to feel hurt and/or anger at the current mood in Germany and in Europe in general. And yet there do remain social organizations and many individuals who embrace difference, migrants, and new cultural experiences. The motives for so doing are often mixed, from mere economic pragmatism to convinced hospitality. Various churches and religious organizations are often at the forefront of such groups, the German United Methodist Church (UMC)[3] being one of them. All that is to say the migrant experience in Germany confronts a deep ambivalence. Places such as these, of ambivalence, can be characterized by *liminality*.[4]

Liminality is, at its most basic, being betwixt and between.[5] Liminality is evident during initiation rituals. People experience liminality when they are neither in the same status as at the beginning nor in the new status of their ending state. For example, as illuminated below, the sacraments are liminal experiences. In baptism, one is changed from old life to new life.

/joachim-herrmann-csu-minister-erklaert-den-wunderbarer-neger-roberto-blanco-satz-a-1050814.html. The Bavarian Interior Minister Joachim Herrmann said this live, on national television, during a roundtable discussion on racism in Germany. He was taking the position that Germany cannot possibly be racist because the singer Roberto Blanco—an African of Tunisian heritage—was a well-loved singer/entertainer. While Herrmann did face popular criticism for his use of the German equivalent of the N-word, he suffered no other consequences and is, of this writing (April 2016), still the Interior Minister of Bavaria in good standing with the CSU party. The N-word in general is used far more commonly in Germany than in, for example, America, and with far less social stigma. It is also not just older people who commonly use it, although it has been removed as a descriptor of certain foods. The continued popular use of the word is symptomatic of Germany's denied and/or ignored colonial heritage, as well as common (and unexaminedly racialist) assumptions about who constitutes a "German." Cf. Grada Kilomba, *Plantation Memories: Episodes of Everyday Racism* (Münster: Unrast, 2008).

3   In German: Evangelisch-methodistische Kirche.

4   Victor Turner, *The Ritual Process: Structure and Anti-Structure* (New Brunswick: Aldine Transaction Press, 2008), 94ff.

5   Turner, *The Ritual Process*, 95.

In the Eucharistic liturgy we speak of being "with all your people on earth and all the company of heaven"[6]—we occupy a space between earth and heaven. Liminality is also evident in the rituals one goes through in order to symbolically become an adult. I use the word *liminality* to describe both the migrant experience and the student university experience, because both can be seen as extended in-between states, not just by their subjects but also by many of those around them and the broader culture. Jung Young Lee and Bernard Adeney-Riskotta rightly point out that migrants, even long-term migrants, are never fully accepted as complete members of the "host" culture.[7] Liminality as Turner described it refers to a transitional space, something neither long-term nor permanent. But for migrants, liminality becomes an extended experience. A transitional space, describing ritual, becomes a longer reality, even permanent, because the sense of dislocation never really goes away although it may sometimes be less noticeable. This dislocation creates a new identity, a "third" identity[8] that is neither German nor Ghanaian, American, Nigerian, Kenyan, and so forth. Jung Young Lee's book on marginality makes a compelling case that migrants experience an extended liminality, one that ceases to be merely transitional. Extending a transitional moment into a long-term, or even a permanent, experience has dislocating effects on those experiencing it. When I refer to liminality within this chapter, I am using Lee's expansion of it as an extended form of liminality unless I otherwise note.

In my ministry context of the German UMC, the experience of migrant liminality is also combined with the experience of students entering university, often with their accompanying families. The university experience as a whole can be described in a basic way as another liminal experience. One is no longer a child in his or her parents' house nor is one necessarily a completely

---

6   *The United Methodist Hymnal* (Nashville: The United Methodist Publishing House, 1989), 9.

7   Jung Young Lee, *Marginality: The Key to Multicultural Ministry* (Minneapolis: Augsburg Fortress Press, 1995), 36–42; Bernard Adeney-Riskotta, *Strange Virtues: Ethics in a Multicultural World* (Downers Grove, IL: InterVarsity Press, 1995), 49.

8   Adeney-Riskotta, *Strange Virtues*, 73.

independent adult. The spouses and children of these students also occupy a difficult space spiritually and culturally speaking. This is especially the case in the context of my ministry where university studies, residency permits, and the lived migrant experience are all tied together. Thus the folks in my ministry experience a "double" liminality. And, because our lived experiences inform our spirituality and vice versa, this double consciousness often manifests in deep feelings of spiritual displacement along with physical and emotional displacement. How does one find a place in such a situation? Or, must we intentionally create a new place?

Having no place, no home, continually feeling uprooted—this is the core of the problem. This is what needs to be addressed. So what are the tools at hand? It is my conviction that our Wesleyan heritage is uniquely equipped to address this problem. First, Wesleyan history offers sympathetic stories, such as John Wesley's encounter with the Moravians on his voyage to America—voyages being another liminal space. Second, Wesleyan theology is a practical theology of personal and social holiness. At the very least, the possibility of some solutions should not be foreign to Wesleyan thought. Third, Wesleyan thought is also ecumenical. John Wesley himself was eminently ecumenical in the interests of holiness. He looked for similarities with Catholics, Calvinists, and others.[9] His practical ecumenism is eminently helpful in ministry contexts where people from many different faith confessions find themselves together in one congregation due to common language. But most important and the focus of this chapter, Wesleyan sacramental theology can act as a unifying and creative ground for migrants and Germans.

My intent is to move from the specific to the general. First, I will share my own story, which will hopefully provide insight into how I relate with and understand the broader German culture and the German UMC. Second, we will move to look at the specifically German, and even more specifically former East German, context. What is the lived reality for myself and similar

---

9   John Wesley, *The Works of the Rev. John Wesley: Volume X* (London: Wesleyan-Methodist Book-Room, 1826), 177–88.

migrants? As Jung Young Lee says, "Theology is certainly autobiographical, because I alone can tell my faith story. However, it is not an autobiography. Telling my story is not itself theology but a basis for theology. . . . This is why one cannot do theology for another. If theology is contextual, it must certainly be at root autobiographical."[10] Or, as Orlando Costas succinctly puts it, "Experience may open up previously undiscovered dimensions of the faith through varied and dynamic events."[11]

With this understanding from Lee and Costas, it is my hope to bring the lens of Wesleyan belief and practice to bear upon my context, so that theological insight may deepen and enrich the kaleidoscopic view of our understanding of God and Church. In this sense I do not believe it is necessary to reinvent the wheel; rather it is my hope to simply follow John Wesley's example: To take established belief and practice and show how it may have practical use for the growth in personal and social holiness, which Methodists profess to be part of Christian perfection. In other words, as with so much else for migrants, it is a matter of translation. Hopefully then we will have some solutions so that the "uprooted plant" will no longer find itself cast upon hostile or apathetic soil but be transplanted into the welcoming, fertile soil of Methodist community.

My Story: Never-Ending Construction

Sometimes I feel like my own story is almost too convoluted to succinctly communicate. Also, I am not much of one for speaking about myself on a personal level, which makes this section of my chapter probably the most difficult one for me. I also sometimes think that if I were to have a patron saint then it must surely be the prophet Jonah, because I continue to find myself doing things that I never wanted nor expected to do. I grew up in Utah, which I still feel is one of the most naturally beautiful places in the world. The landscape truly shaped me in more ways than I am even aware

---

10 Lee, *Marginality*, 7.

11 Orlando Costas, *Liberating News: A Theology of Contextual Evangelism* (Eugene: Wipf and Stock, 1989), 6.

of, to the point that I never wanted to live anywhere without mountains. Yet, somehow I found myself in northern Germany and furthermore in a part of northern Germany where they call the smallest hills mountains.

My wife is German, which explains my big move from the United States to Germany, where I found myself in a totally foreign culture and completely dislocated from all cultural touchstones. Very few of the people in the city where I moved to spoke English. On the one hand this had the positive effect of forcing me to learn German quickly. On the other this made for a few very lonely years. Shortly after I moved to Germany, the German UMC asked me to take over an English-language ministry in Cottbus. Like many migrant congregations, the Cottbus congregation is rather poor but quite lively. A couple of years after I started in Cottbus, I was asked if I would consider working in a German-language congregation as well. I currently split my time between the two.

The German UMC is somewhat small in number, with only around sixty thousand members and without any state connection such as that found with the Lutheran or Catholic churches. We are a "free church," which means that we are poorer, but we often have higher rates of lay participation. However, my experience of the German UMC is that it, like all churches, is enculturated. Many of the common assumptions that Germans make, assumptions that I as someone who is not German do not share, are also found in the pews and pulpits of the German UMC. I say this in the most neutral way. Culture is neither uniformly bad nor uniformly good. Nor is the enculturated nature of churches necessarily a bad thing, as long as the awareness of enculturation is there—as long as there exists the realization that the gospel transcends all cultures and is not synonymous with any particular culture. That, however, is not always the case.

My experiences in ministry sometimes leave me feeling quite ambivalent. I enjoy serving both congregations, even though I feel like quite the circuit rider when I travel 200 kilometers to my congregation in Cottbus. The German congregation I serve in is also the church in which my wife is assigned, so it is my home congregation. Without the German congregation I think my first few years in Germany would have been even more difficult than they were. But the broader church structures and my experiences at district meetings and annual conferences tend not to reflect the joys of local church ministry, which I suppose is probably true for most people.

But it is in these broader settings that I continue to encounter moments of spiritual and emotional dislocation. There have been many times when I have heard a colleague at a meeting speak about "foreigners" or even "Americans" in very general terms. On the one hand this means that my colleague has likely accepted me as functionally "German." On the other hand, I am still a foreigner by German law and common German thinking. I am spoken about in general terms, and in the third person, either as if I am not there or as if I somehow do not count. What is my role in such moments? Am I German? A foreigner? Something else? Or, perhaps the speaker has merely forgotten that her or his words are relevant to myself, possibly because I look "German," which is to say that I am white. Such words, which most likely come from an inexact carelessness rather than spite, have the effect of pushing me out of the collegial "we" and into "the other." I am not German. I am a foreigner. If my colleague is being dismissive, then am I dismissed? How do we speak, and what assumptions do we make, when we are in a group of people? Do we assume that everyone is like us, the speaker?

Sometimes these experiences are more amusing to me than dislocating, at least at first. There was one instance when I was sitting in on a senior's meeting and the theme was prejudice. During the meeting, one person replied that some prejudices are true, and they stated as an example that all Americans are fat. I, frequently reminded by my health insurance that I am *underweight*, was sitting right next to this person at the time, and they knew that I was an American. Then someone else pointed out that I, a thin person, was sitting right beside the speaker. I suppose the theme of prejudice was quite relevant that day.

Such experiences serve to remind me of my constant feeling of dislocation in Germany. Sometimes the sensations of dislocation are small and manageable. Other times they increase. It is a fluctuating spectrum where I become more or less German, more or less American, but never really either anymore. This has been very useful for my ministry, in that my space as neither/nor helps me to critique the areas where my own Christian understanding has been negatively mixed with culture. But it has also been challenging, because many cultural references that I make in sermons are simply not from a shared language.

The result of my experiences seems to be that my theology is constantly experiencing growth, destruction, deconstruction, and new growth. On a purely intellectual level, I can see this as something both good and natural. Change is a sign of growth and, hopefully, hints toward a growth in Wesleyan perfection. It has perhaps also made me a bit mercenary in the sources I use for theological de/construction. At the same time the changing nature of my theology is unsettling. Sometimes it is nice just to have some kind of stability, some kind of foundation—especially for a migrant who may have little to no stability in other areas. Does this mean migrants live their entire lives coping with instability? For many migrants, exhaustion from this tension is a daily reality. Perhaps I did not sit down to count out the cost before building the tower, to recall Jesus's parable, but certainly one could say that there is never a dull moment. Some days I think I cannot possibly go on, and other days I think I could never do anything else. That is probably why, as I said at the beginning of this section, I often feel a certain affection for the prophet Jonah.

The Wider German Context

To understand the more general German cultural context, one has to consider both a general Western European perspective and a specifically German one. In many ways Germany mirrors much of how the West has interacted with migrants and the topic of migration. But, in other key ways, Germany is somewhat unique. It occupies a middle place in Europe, a placement that goes back hundreds of years and has as its most recent example Germany's split into two countries at the end of World War II. It is, in many ways, both generally West and somewhat different.

German reaction to migrants and migration has often been a reaction filled with racism. This includes the perspective that migrant individuals cease to be *individuals* and become mere representatives of their entire culture or ethnicity.[12] Yet, as Manchala and coauthors point out, the expression of racism is also changing in Europe today. "Some researchers suggest that racism has changed in the twentieth and twenty-first centuries from an overt, more blatant manifestation of discrimination and harassment to a more covert, hidden or generally more sophisticated form which stresses cultural incompatibility and the exclusion of migrants and asylum seekers, whilst portraying extremist groups such as the British National Party or the National Front as being the true racists."[13] Further, "This low-level racism, like the dropping of water on a stone, can often do more to erode a sense of being a whole and acceptable person because of its persistence and ubiquitousness."[14]

This two-pronged form of racism has recently become more pronounced in German society. A group called Pegida (Patriotic Europeans against the "Islamification" of the West) has grown in response to the influx of Syrian refugees.[15] Overtly racist signs are common at their rallies. The boundaries between this group and outright neo-Nazis and other violent right-wing groups are hard to draw. On the other hand, a new political party called the Alternative for Germany (AfD) has grown. This group had its start as a Euro-skeptic group in reaction to the bailouts of Greece. But, after a fight for leadership, they have morphed into a party that has capitalized on discontent over the refugee influx in Germany. They received up to 24 percent of the vote in recent state elections in spite of not even having a party platform other than the common knowledge that they are antiforeigner.

Still, it often remains difficult to truly separate "new" racism from "old" racism. Two prominent AfD leaders have stated that refugees should be shot at the borders of Germany. The overlap between AfD and Pegida is

---

12 Deenabandhu Manchala, Drea Frtchtling, and Michael Trice, *Cruelty and Christian Witness* (Geneva: WCC Publications, 2011), 14.

13 Manchala et al., 16.

14 Manchala et al., 17. Cf. Kilomba, *Plantation Memories*.

15 Ironically enough, Pegida is most popular in the state of Saxony, which has had the smallest amount of refugees resettled out of all sixteen federal German states.

noticeable. So, rather than two distinct strains, Germany is experiencing more of a mishmash of racism. The current state is that of nebulous and not so nebulous groups, where membership overlaps, which spans the spectrum from purely "new" racist thinking to "old" racism. Furthermore, as far back as 1982, this "new" form of racism was already making its way into the German mainstream. A group of academics published what was called the "Heidelberger Manifesto," where they clearly state their fear of the foreigner: "The integration of large masses of non-German foreigners is not possible without threatening the German people, language, culture, and religion."[16] For a group of academics, it is astonishing that they seem to assume that language, culture, and religion are all static realities that never experience change. The economist and politician Thilo Sarrazin became famous, or infamous, with a book he wrote a few years back titled *Germany Does Away with Itself.*[17] In this work he argued that Turkish people were inherently incapable of integrating into German culture. Indeed, his book came so close to arguing scientific racism based on "genetics" that it almost fell afoul of anti-Nazi laws. His political party, the Social Democratic Party of Germany (SPD), which currently rules in coalition, started a process to eject him from the party. That process failed, and he remains in the party and has since written further works with similar themes.

"New" racist rhetoric seeks to hide itself behind a veneer of objectivity. This goes beyond the scientism of Thilo Sarrazin and the concerned sociology of the "Heidelberger Manifesto." *Es muss gesagt werden* (It must be said) is the opening phrase that signifies something in the strain of the "new racism" is about to be said. *Must* it really be said? Or is it a clever phrase that distances the speaker from anything unsavory that she or he actually says? Furthermore, the complaint "If you criticize the current policy [regarding refugees] then you get called racist" has also become a beloved phrase.

---

16 Deniz Göktürk, *Germany in Transit: Nation and Migration 1955–2005* (Berkeley: University of California Press, 2007), 112.

17 *Deutschland schafft sich ab.*

Curiously enough, in my experience, the people who use these phrases the most are also the people most likely to say blatantly racist things.

So, while it is true that this newer form of racism has become prevalent in Germany and Europe in general, it has not spelled the demise of the older form of overt, violent racism. Ute Andresen noted in 1999, "The chances of becoming a victim of a xenophobic attack between Rostock and Cottbus are high—27 times higher than in the West [the former West Germany]."[18] The instances of violent attacks have only increased as of late, especially with the most recent arrival of hundreds of thousands of Syrian refugees.[19] Arson of refugee shelters has become the common program of violent racists.

With this context in mind, it is important to note where Germany differs from other Western European countries. Deenabandhu Manchala notes that the roots of modern racism are found in the European colonial project.[20] But Germany has a far different experience of colonialism than France or England. It is true that Germany joined the colonial project. Cynically enough, they termed their colonies "Protected Areas."[21] Until the end of World War I Germany controlled Cameroon, Tanzania, Namibia, Togoland, parts of New Guinea and Samoa, ports in China, and surrounding areas of these colonies. Yet many Germans are only aware of their colonial past in the vaguest way. In German history, the tragedy of World War II and the Holocaust overshadow World War I and the previous colonial projects. The former colonies simply fail to register in general for Germans today. There was never a steady migration from the colonies to Germany such as in France/Algeria or England/India. Because Germany only kept its colonies for roughly forty years, the assumption is that this part of their history is of

---

18 Göktürk, *Germany in Transit*, 133. Conveniently enough, the cities of Rostock and Cottbus respectively represent the northern- and southernmost parts of the Berlin District of the North German Annual Conference, which is entirely within the former East. My ministry with migrants is in the city of Cottbus.

19 "'Hart aber fair' zu Fremdenhass: Ach ja, diese besorgten Bürger," *Der Spiegel*, 1 December 2015, accessed 11 May 2016, http://www.spiegel.de/kultur/tv/hart-aber-fair-mit-frank-plasberg-ach-ja-diese -besorgten-buerger-a-1065367.html.

20 Manchala et al., *Cruelty and Christian Witness*, 13.

21 *Schutzgebiete*.

little importance. Interdisciplinary artist and writer Grada Kilomba notes this fact when she asks her class what happened in Berlin in 1888. Her white German students are unable to answer the question, but her students of African heritage know that the Berlin Conference in 1888 was a meeting of the colonial powers to carve up spheres of influence in Africa. The end result was that, by the time of World War I, only Liberia and Ethiopia remained independent.

The general ignorance of Germany's colonial history is a shame, but it also hides the fact that racial thinking from the colonial project made its way into German society at that time. It hides the fact that Germany's colonial past helped pave the way for the racialist and racist ideologies of Nazism. It hides the fact that racism is still part of the German consciousness when it comes to discussion of "what makes a person German." Unlike France or England, where there are large groups of nonwhite citizens, Germany has not historically had this experience. Nonwhite citizens exist but remain a minority, either ignored or treated with apathy. This ignorance and apathy underlie the more blatant racism, both "old" and "new." To cite a statement from the Christian Social Union (CSU) party (again, part of the governing coalition) from 2004, "Germany is not a classic country of immigration, and because of its history, geography, and economic conditions, it cannot be one."[22]

The apathy of Germany toward foreigners is perhaps best seen in the fact that, for decades, the political response to the issues of migration was merely ad hoc.[23] The need for comprehensive work was not seen. The colonial history was buried under the trauma of the Nazi era. However, an apathetic response is by no means specifically German in nature. Deenabandhu Manchala notes, "The importance of dealing justly with foreigners and people of ethnically different origins does not seem to have formed a prominent feature of any of the European legal or moral systems up until the present

---

22 Göktürk, *Germany in Transit*, 4.

23 Göktürk, 3.

day."[24] Again, Deniz Göktürk points out that Germany generally does not even distinguish between the various forms of migrants. There are multiple forms of residency, and various groups have settled in Germany since the end of World War II and the fall of the Berlin Wall, with Russian Germans and Turks being two of the largest groups. However, regardless of one's residency status or place of origin, there is just one word used for description: foreigner (*Ausländer*),[25] often used in a pejorative sense.[26] The problem of using one word as a catch-all is compounded by the fact that Germany does not grant automatic citizenship to people born in Germany. This means that there are second- and third-generation people with a migrant background who are still considered "Italian" or "Turks." It does not matter that they were born and raised in Germany, as their parents were, and possibly even their grandparents. It does not matter that their mother tongue, and sometimes their only language, is German. They remain citizens of another country, *Ausländer*. Thinking about what it means to be a foreigner to those around you while living in what is effectively your own country is rare. If such thoughts do not stem from experiencing the hostility of others then they can only stem from the ignorance and/or apathy of others.

This is a broad outline of general German action and reaction, but it only highlights and does not do justice to the migrant experience. Especially in the context of young adult ministry in Cottbus. We need to become even more specific. We need to discuss how the former East and West Germany still remain very different contexts. I mentioned above the prevalence of Pegida in the eastern state of Saxony and the higher likelihood of being attacked if you lived in Brandenburg, Berlin, or Mecklenburg-Vorpommern around the turn of the millennium. Even after twenty-five years, the former East and the former West have many differences. Reunification is a process, and it is one that has not always gone smoothly or justly. In spite of what optimists may

---

24 Manchala, et al., *Cruelty and Christian Witness*, 21.

25 The plural form is also *Ausländer*.

26 Göktürk, *Germany in Transit*, 4. Subsequent citations to this source found two paragraphs down and are noted parenthetically in the text, by page number.

think or hope, it is a continuing process. But the pessimists are not correct if they claim that nothing has truly changed and/or nothing ever will. Much has changed, much has remained the same. Along with that, the experience in cities differs from the experience in smaller towns.

Even though Germany has been reunified for over two decades now, the ramifications of the reunification continue to be felt. A separation of almost sixty years cannot be so easily wiped away either politically or culturally. In spite of the new openness and the ability to freely travel, certain attitudes remain entrenched and even get passed on as part of the cultural store to the next generations. Certain attitudes common to the former East make ministry here far different, and oftentimes far more difficult, than in the former West. Chief among these is simply the fact of having been effectively "shut off" from the rest of the world for decades. For example, as one expert noted, the former GDR lacked a culture of discussion. "There was no talk of unpleasant things and no debate on the past" (134). The new right-wing extremism in the former East can also be attributed to the culture of upbringing. "The Socialist Unity Party state reared its citizens to become conformist, dependent subjects who long for strong leadership and vent their aggressions on foreigners" (133). This has led to what some have titled the "New Wall," one that no longer exists only in Berlin (139). The end result is a distrust of the "foreigner" deep in the soul of the German nation—even deeper in the former East. "When he [a foreigner] has assimilated himself and conformed, he can be all the more dangerous and could weaken and betray us from within" (213).

All of this results in both outright evil, observed in the far-right acts of violence, and in what Ken Booth describes as "social evil." That is, an evil created and perpetuated by bureaucratic systems where the individual human actors in the systems are disconnected from their own moral obligations through the obligation to continue the system. It is an evil that becomes faceless and heartless, not because it is spiteful but because it is merely apathetic.[27]

---

27 Ken Booth, *How Might We Live? Global Ethics in the New Century* (Cambridge: Cambridge University Press, 2001), 77.

The Construction/Maintaining of an Identity in the German Liminal Reality

The young people participating in the ministries in Cottbus, Germany, are mostly there to study at the Brandenburg Technical University. However, quite a few people are also family members and children who have since been born in Germany. This creates a further tension, as the family members are often not allowed to work or study in Germany. They are merely there as "dependents" of the one studying. Just as the university students often exist in a place between adolescent dependency and the freedom of adult working life, so their family members exist between their earlier independence in their birth country and their current dependency in Germany. In their birth country, they were able to hold jobs, study, or engage in any other endeavors open to them. In Germany, they are not. And if they want to be able to study or work in Germany, then they have to go through the social evils of German bureaucracy. Whereas students find some sense of community and belonging in the fellowship of students, their families may struggle to a greater extent. The questions of identity are raised and struggled with in a context of greater or lesser displacement.

As previously mentioned, this displacement, or liminality, is not meant to be a permanent or long-term state.[28] Leslie Adelson criticizes it as a sort of "reservation," meant to hold certain people, knowledge, and experiences in abeyance rather than enable.[29] Bernard Adeney-Riskotta agrees by labeling this liminal stage a "transitional" one, noting that in this period the excitement of a foreigner being "exotic" has worn off and gets replaced by a cooler reception.[30] Nevertheless, this "temporary" phase is often drawn out. One never fully leaves such a stage, because one never truly arrives. A migrant, even one who has gone through the process of attaining German citizenship, still remains in the position of having grown up somewhere else,

---

28 Turner, *The Ritual Process*, 94.

29 Göktürk, *Germany in Transit*, 266.

30 Adeney-Riskotta, *Strange Virtues*, 134.

of having absorbed the cultural values, landmarks, and norms of another place. While a migrant can slowly learn cultural references, there is always one more to learn. It is never really enough. In fact, I have known many Germans to describe migrants who have since attained German citizenship in terms of the country from which they originate. For example, some people, even if they have lived in Germany for decades, are perpetually known as "so-and-so, the Indian." The migrant never truly arrives, because the broader culture still insists on locating him or her somewhere else. The migrant becomes a liminal person.[31] Again, while Turner speaks of liminal people in the context of short-term rituals, for migrants liminality is a long-term experience.

However, one can reach a point where some form of equilibrium has been achieved. As Miroslav Volf points out, distance from one's own culture should make the fluidity and hybridity of culture livable,[32] because distance helps one to realize that culture is not as monolithic as we sometimes assume it to be. All cultures are hybrids and oftentimes distance is the best tool for being able to recognize that. I believe the same point can be made for a host culture as well. At some point, distance makes it possible to live with the uncertainty of culture. This is the gift of liminality. "The strangeness of strangers is their greatest asset."[33] A difficult asset, to be sure, but one with many rewards. As Zafer Senocak points out, "Every border separates and joins at the same time."[34]

So how does one go about constructing and maintaining an identity on such slippery grounds? Especially in a Christian, and specifically Wesleyan, context in the former East Germany? Can anything be built, or is this just another exercise of building castles on sand? I think the answer lies in this perspective: The Christian and Wesleyan context can serve as a foundation

---

31 Turner, *The Ritual Process*, 95.

32 Miroslav Volf, *Von der Ausgrenzung zur Umarmung* (Marburg an der Lahn: Francke-Buchhandlung GmbH, 2012), 60.

33 Adeney-Riskotta, *Strange Virtues*, 138.

34 Göktürk, *Germany in Transit*, 238.

while the interaction between this foundation and cultural interaction must remain flexible and open to change. How much is foundation, and how much is up for reevaluation and reinterpretation? Or, to put it another way, what is gospel and what is culture? Miroslav Volf rightly points out that our duties as Christians and our cultural duties are far too often intermixed.[35] So where do we begin to base identity in such a context? What can we set as a foundation for this "third identity" that is neither American, Ghanaian, Nigerian, Indian, Korean, nor German?

The easy answer would be simply to say that our identity is found in Christ. Enough of all these complicated cultural identities; we are focusing entirely on the wrong thing and, possibly, engaging in idolatry at the same time! It is easy enough, and even true enough, to say that our identity is, or should be, founded in Christ. However, such an answer is too simplistic. It is mere cliché and an empty truism, akin to telling a sick person that "everything happens for a reason." In other words, it is theologizing a truism and trying to shield oneself from the complexities of life. In other words, it is a functionally useless statement by itself. However, it is one that migrants sometimes hear when discussing the difficulty of occupying a liminal space.

A better starting point would be to say, with Josef Pieper, that Christ is our exemplar.[36] This is quite different from the assertion that our identity is "found in Christ." Pieper's wording allows for the reality that some, or much, of our identity may *not* be found in Christ but rather found in our culture. Whereas the truism above represents an end to a conversation, Pieper's statement represents a beginning. "Christ is our exemplar." This challenges us to ask where we go from here; how can we model Christ in our lives? The natural progression from Pieper's statement and my following questions would be to posit something that we should do. We should act selflessly, for example, or pray more, or take some action in order to more closely be like Christ.

---

35 Volf, *Von der Ausgrenzung zur Umarmung*, 40.

36 Josef Pieper, *The Christian Idea of Man* (South Bend: St. Augustine's Press, 2011), 5.

However, this immediate jump to doing ignores the fact that migrants are already doing many things in the liminal space. It also ignores something more fundamental to our own imitation of Christ in the realm of ethical interaction with one another: being. As Pieper says, "People should not think so much about what they ought to do; they should think about what they ought to be."[37] This is not to deny that what we do contributes to identity; rather Pieper is reordering how we as Christians should ethically think. Pieper's refocusing of ethical interaction and our imitation of Christ to include the sphere of being is vital for the construction of an identity in liminal space. The migrant in Germany, for example, is already doing much to try to accommodate herself to a foreign culture. Surrounded by Germans, it seems to her that she is *only* doing and that her actions minimize or even mask her true self. Often migrants wear either a mask of outward conformity or a mask of interesting exoticness. In either case, these actions keep migrants from being who they truly are.

From the other side—that is, the actions of German individuals and groups—there is also a lot of doing. Well-intentioned people establish round tables, sports clubs invite people in, churches try to adjust their ecclesiological structures to migrant congregations, and so on. While all this doing may be, more or less, changing the attitudes (being) of the participants, it fails to address the root differences, becoming a mere facade of obligation. Hence doing can come to take priority over being to the point where even the doing itself can become part of Booth's critique of social evil. Doing at the expense of being can result in a heartless charity or a mask that hides our own personal core behind others' expectations or demands.

Especially in a migrant context, it is time to include more intentionally being with doing. This is a far more challenging proposition than simply starting up a new welcome table or conforming to social mores that we hardly understand, because a focus on ethical being requires introspection, self-criticism, and a distance from one's own culture.[38] It is this last step that

---

37 Pieper, *Christian Idea*, 4.

38 Volf, *Von der Ausgrenzung zur Umarmung*, 58.

can be the most difficult for migrants. Coming into a new culture, where everything is unknown, can create a tendency for migrants to cling to their ideas of the "home" culture even more; at least the home culture is something a migrant is familiar with. It provides an anchor in a storm. But one's home culture remains simply the home culture; if one clings desperately to it he or she is not free to take Christ as exemplar. We must be free and open to the new possibilities that will present themselves.

So what can a migrant to Cottbus, Germany, be? What can a migrant in any country be? What being is there to find in a liminal space? Again, we can turn back to Pieper's succinct statement of Christ being our exemplar. The liminal space is precisely where we can find Christ. Jesus Christ, who was born to an unwed mother, fled as a refugee to Egypt, grew up in the backwaters of Israel, departed into the desert for forty days, wandered and taught as an itinerant rabbi without a home, was rejected by his own people, and was crucified as an outcast by the Romans. When we look at the life of Jesus Christ, we find plenty of liminality in his story. His story can show that our own liminality does not have to be devoid of God's presence and that it can give us greater opportunity to be Christ for others.

Arriving at a Wesleyan Theology of Baptism

Furthermore, the migrants in my Cottbus ministry either come to Germany as baptized Christians or are baptized here. Baptism is, in the Wesleyan tradition, a sacrament whereby we accept God's gift of a grace-filled ontological change in our being. It is, as Ted Runyon says, "a renewal of the image of God in humankind."[39] God renews our being, whatever our immigration status, to conform to the imago Dei. Baptism is the promise of Galatians 3:28 made concrete: "There is no longer Jew or Greek, there is no longer slave or free, there is no longer male and female; for all of you are one in Christ Jesus." Our being, because we are baptized Christians, has been changed, and as

---

39 Ted Runyon, *The New Creation: John Wesley's Theology Today* (Nashville: Abingdon Press, 1998), 140.

migrants we have the opportunity to experience a fuller meaning of Paul's words. While Germany may still insist that there are Germans and *Ausländer*, our baptism reminds us that our being is beyond such worldly distinctions.

What Ted Runyon succinctly expressed is expanded in John Wesley's treatise on baptism, which has useful insights for the migrant experience in Germany. Wesley writes that baptism is "the initiatory sacrament" that brings us into a covenant with God.[40] Wesley reiterates the nature of baptism as a covenant shortly after, and expands his description of baptism to an "everlasting covenant."[41] The nature of baptism as covenant is important for both migrants and nonmigrants. In the Bible, the covenant is the primary responsibility, the foundation upon which all identity and worldview are built. Baptism, as a covenant for Methodist Christians, supersedes all else, especially cultural understandings and national identity.

John Wesley does not just speak of baptism in juristic terms, like *covenant*, either. That is merely one aspect of the Methodist understanding of baptism. But mixed within the juridical understanding is also a mystical understanding. Wesley quotes the baptismal office and declares baptism an "everlasting benediction of [God's] heavenly washing."[42] This is what Runyon translates as a renewal of the image of God. The renewal comes about by the blessing (benediction), which is God's gift to us, and washes our marred image clean. But Wesley is not finished with his mystical language just yet. He goes on to make the sacramental nature of baptism even clearer: The baptized are "mystically united to Christ, and made one with him."[43] Furthermore, this union is not just with Christ, but we become "members" of the body of Christ. Our union is also with the Church[44]—with each other, again, regardless of the distinctions that we still like to cling to.

---

40 John Wesley, "A Treatise on Baptism," in *The Works of the Rev. John Wesley, A.M., Sometime Fellow of Lincoln College, Oxford* (London: Wesleyan-Methodist Book-Room), I.1.

41 Wesley, "Treatise on Baptism," II.2.

42 Wesley, "Treatise on Baptism," II.1.

43 Wesley, "Treatise on Baptism," II.3.

44 Wesley, "Treatise on Baptism," II.3.

The baptismal change is a direct challenge to the daily lived experience of migrants and all people. The Wesleyan theology of baptism points us toward what Miroslav Volf calls the "un-ethnicization" of religion, because we profess it as a sacrament from God and a change in our being away from worldly distinctions.[45] This challenges not just the German UMC structures and its cultural Christianity but also the migrant Christian coming into Germany. Migrants also bring in an ethnicized Christianity. All too often, we migrants prefer to self-segregate into religioethnic ghettos where we can feel spiritually comfortable. Our baptismal change of being can challenge this impulse within migrants as well. Paul's words in Galatians are not just a critique that we can level at the host culture but also words that challenge us as Christians and migrants.

Our being, as baptized Christians, can conform to a renewed image of God—an exemplar of Christ. This is not a comfortable status for any of us so long as cultural norms permeate any church, and religioethnic ghettoization remains the response of migrants. In this sense, we all fail at living up to the promise of God that Paul communicates in Galatians. Additionally, we all fail at living out our Wesleyan heritage. However, pointing out the failures on both sides is not the same as claiming that they are equal. To the credit of the German UMC and the migrant congregations, these failures are becoming acknowledged on both sides, which is challenging all of us to move beyond the status quo. Some of what has been done on both sides is in the process of being undone as it becomes recognized as a failure to live up to the promise of baptism. And the focus on our being as Christians is slowly coming to the fore. Still, migrants and Germans occupy unequal spaces in terms of power both in broader German culture and in more specifically Christian contexts. It is true that we have, as Orlando Costas says, both "sinned and sinned against,"[46] but that is not to say that the sins are equal in scope or effect. Our common baptism challenges us to become closer to

---

45 Volf, *Von der Ausgrenzung zur Umarmung*, 56.

46 Costas, *Liberating News*, 22.

one another—to truly *be* the body of the baptized over merely continuing to do the haphazard and clumsy actions that we have both been doing.

For this to continue to happen, we need to realize that our common baptism brings us not just into a common family but also into dialogue with each other. Yet, even here, we still run into the problem of unequal power. So we still must be very careful with how we engage in dialogue with one another. Jung Young Lee says that the Church should exist as a "marginal community."[47] That is, the Church should follow her Lord Jesus Christ into the margins, into liminality, into powerlessness. Rather than seeking to move to the center, the Church should seek to move to the margins. This is especially important for those who already have power within the Church but also, in light of intersectionality, important for those who have less power within the Church. Perhaps this means that the voices that have been dominant in the German UMC need to be still for a time and listen. On the other hand, those with less power cannot simply recreate the structures that they know from their countries of origin. Migrant women, for example, can find themselves marginalized both by the German UMC and their own migrant congregations. Seek the margins; make it a guiding movement for dialogue.

Secondly, dialogue between any enculturated church and migrants should seek to focus on engaging with the truth. This may seem self-evident but it is not. There is a qualitative difference between a dialogue that seeks the truth together and a dialogue where one party seeks to convince the other party of its rightness. In fact, in the second case, it ceases to be a dialogue altogether and becomes a monologue. This dialogue needs to be ongoing and not simply a reaction to culture clashes within congregations or at church events. The seeking of truth is a communal effort requiring the presence of both those in the center and those in the margins. "Truth lives in dialogue, in discussion, in conversation."[48] We can move beyond enculturated Christianity only through interactions with Christians from other cultures. It takes

---

47 Lee, *Marginality*, 153.

48 Josef Pieper, *Abuse of Language—Abuse of Power* (San Francisco: Ignatius Press, 1992), 36.

an outside view to be able to see just how "inside" we are. Without such a view, without marginal voices, we will remain possessing only a partial truth at best. We will remain baptized into the family, but we may lack the fullness of the image of God—"Christian perfection," as John Wesley put it.

Seeking truth in dialogue is not easy, though. It is not easy to give up our agendas and ideas. After all, we have some pretty good ideas. We know how to get things done and what others should do. But that is merely setting the goal of dialogue a few steps short of the truth, at a specific goal. This is not to say that such goals are inherently *bad*, merely that they keep us from the fullness of truth, the exemplar of Christ, the being in fullness. Being in dialogue is another way to practice marginality. It can be a marginal act to be quiet and listen rather than to dominate the conversation. It can be an act of decentering to put others on an equal level as yourself. With Jesus's words, "I am the Way, the Truth, and the Life,"[49] and remembering Jesus's own life of liminality, we discover that the truth is deeply tied to the margins.

Dialogue in search of truth is something we can do out of the realization of our changed being through baptism. But, dialogue in search of truth is also something that can affect our being, not just through the repositioning of ourselves away from the center and toward the margins but because it changes that web of relationships among migrant and German Christians. But even further, it changes and *heals* the relationships that exist between migrant and German Christians. It heals what is, ultimately, the one Body of Christ—the Church. As Pope Francis said in his beautiful encyclical *Laudato Si'*, "Hell ends when people come into community and relationships of interdependency."[50] Our interactions with each other, the broader world, and all of creation around us can lead us to experience an ontological change through dialogue in search of truth.

We can see already how things are intertwined: baptism leads to dialogue which leads to healing. The ontological change of our being in baptism leads to our own doing in dialogue with one another, and then to the change in

---

49 John 14:6, NRSV.

50 Pope Francis, *Enzyklika Laudato Si'* (Bonn: Libreria Editrice Vaticana, 2015), 107.

our being wrought by healing. We can also see now why Josef Pieper's insistence on being over doing is so important. For dialogue to search out truth, there needs to be a preparedness in those participating. There needs to be some kind of common ground that, in the Christian and Wesleyan context, baptism can provide. With baptism, and the focus on changed being, put properly in the foreground, then a chain is formed where one link informs and empowers the next. But there is still one more link in this chain in order to have a properly Wesleyan fullness of insight.

A Wesleyan Theology of the Eucharist

If baptism changes our being and brings us into a dialogue in the search of truth, then the sacrament of the Eucharist deepens the dialogue. It is an ever-renewing source of forgiveness and grace. It is an always-available place where we can come together as equals. It is also a place that challenges us to come together as equals. It marginalizes us all by putting God at the center. It challenges us to rethink our entire world and our perceived place in it. It is a place where we "gather with all the company of saints," not just those saints who look like us, think like us, and come from our own culture. The Eucharist is the liminal space par excellence, in that it reminds us that our entire existence in this world is but a migrant's experience, that we are all strangers in a strange land.

This means that, for migrants, we are experiencing a sort of double liminality when we participate in Communion. We are already experiencing the extended liminality, which I defined above. But we are also experiencing the short-term Turnerian liminality within a ritual. Incidentally, the same holds true for when migrants go through the ritual of baptism. In both instances we are liminal beings who go through another process that includes liminal moments. While Jung Young Lee does not address this double liminality in his book, he does come up with a term that I think also applies to this situation: "the margins of marginality."[51] It is precisely within the margins of

---

51 Lee, *Marginality*, 77ff.

marginality where Lee finds Jesus Christ to be fully present. What he then terms "the creative core," which he also separates from "the center," is where the powerful dwell.[52] It is also in the sacraments where we regularly meet Jesus Christ. First in baptism, and more regularly in Communion.

This is one of the effects of Communion as a "converting ordinance."[53] It does not just act in saving us from our sins; it also acts in converting our very way of thinking. It converts our entire worldview. Along with baptism, it causes an ontological change within us. It shifts us into marginality, away from the center yet into the creative core. John Wesley describes Communion as "the present strengthening and refreshing of our souls."[54] The center is not the natural place for our souls to be. We are not the center. The Communion liturgy reminds us that we are not the center. It challenges us to move to the margins. When there, we can find the strengthening and refreshment we need, because it takes a lot of work to keep ourselves in the center. It takes a lot of work to gain and keep power. It wearies our souls, whether we realize it or not. This is one of the reasons why Wesley recommended "constant" Communion. This is also why the Methodist Communion table remains a place of radical openness to all. Wesley realized our tendency to weary ourselves, that this tendency begins early on and can negatively shape our lives. Furthermore, Communion leads us on to perfection, which is the goal for all.[55] Constant Communion does not just change our sinful practices, it effects a change within us by its refreshment and decentering. Communion changes us to be like God (at the margin of marginality) in holiness.[56]

While we partake of Communion, we are surrounded by that "great cloud of saints." But Communion also supports us in our efforts toward

---

52 Lee, 96.

53 Runyon, *The New Creation*, 134.

54 John Wesley, "The Duty of Constant Communion," in *The Works of the Rev. John Wesley, A.M., Sometime Fellow of Lincoln College, Oxford* (London: Wesleyan-Methodist Book-Room), I.2.

55 Wesley, "Duty of Constant Communion," I.3.

56 Wesley, "Duty of Constant Communion," II.5.

becoming renewed images of God. Baptism is a one-time change in our being but Communion is a continuing change. Because of all of this, Communion can help deepen the already-begun dialogue. If we already acknowledge our one common baptism—the wiping away of Jew and Greek, slave and free, male and female—as something that can draw us together in order to search for truth beyond cultural codes, then Communion can be a present and regular means to reinforce this. Communion can enhance and deepen the dialogue. It can be a regular humbling of ourselves. It can regularly tear down the walls we like to build out of comfort by insisting that God issues the invitation to the Table. Communion is a valuable course-corrector to those human interactions that so readily and easily drift away from their purpose. It is during Communion that we encounter truth, and that our hunger for truth is whetted again.

Miroslav Volf speaks of Christianity as requiring a change of loyalty from the culture and its gods to the God over all cultures.[57] Communion is one of the means by which this loyalty change is demanded. In the liturgy of Communion we make our prayer of confession and our commitment to repentance. We may fail at embodying the change of loyalty that Communion demands but, through regularly receiving Communion as a means of grace, we can trust that it will continue to work as God has promised. We can trust that it will, slowly but surely, continue to cause a change in our very being. That someday, our loyalty will no longer be in question, that we will no longer find it an effort to decentralize ourselves and work together in the dialogue searching for truth. In this way, Communion acts very similarly to baptism in that it deepens the dialogue and facilitates healing.

Location, Location, Location

These two processes, of (1) baptism leading to dialogue leading to healing, and (2) Communion leading to dialogue leading to healing, never take place in a vacuum, although, up until now, I have spoken about them in

---

57 Volf, *Von der Ausgrenzung zur Umarmung*, 44.

fairly general terms. But, as Orlando Costas reminds us, theology is always a contextual endeavor.[58] I spoke at the beginning of "hostile soil." That was not just a convenient metaphor for the reality of migrants in Germany. I am convinced that geography plays a much greater role in both theology and our own individual spiritual formation than we realize. Pope Francis in his encyclical *Laudato Si'* acknowledges this by noting that the story of our friendship with God always begins in a particular geographical space.[59] Furthermore, our geographical surroundings are important for a healthy and integrated understanding of our own identity.[60] These statements from the Pope reveal an entirely different and often ignored facet of migrant experience. We say migrant persons are persons who have left their homeland, but that is not just leaving friends and family in the old neighborhood, because migrants leave deeper and more complex connections.

All Christians are baptized and raised in a particular geographical context. Yet, migrants find themselves in another particular geographical context upon entering Germany. How is this sense of spiritual-geographical dislocation to be handled? How does a Wesleyan view of the sacraments of baptism and the Eucharist impact the lived experience of migrants? How does the theoretical meet the practical? If it truly were so simple as to meditate on our being and connect with the Wesleyan sacraments, then why are there still so many obstacles? Why is the soil still so scattered with hostility, even occasionally within the German UMC?

Clearly it is not enough simply to intellectually grasp the knowledge that our baptism has created a new Being. Nor is it enough to intellectually grasp the radical inclusion of the Wesleyan Table. These teachings need to find their place not just in our heads, but in our hearts, which are often enculturated over decades with other assumptions about Jews and Greeks, slaves and free, males and females. Baptism and the Eucharist are our new reality, but the new reality still struggles with the old reality. That

---

58 Costas, *Liberating News*, 10.

59 Pope Francis, *Enzyklika Laudato Si'*, 62.

60 Pope Francis, 107.

requires regular work from us as we seek to live out the promises of our sacraments. Both Germans and migrants are called to a greater faithfulness in being the Church.

It is a common saying for many Germans that "integration is a two-way street." There is truth to this saying. It is also true that many migrant congregations fail to think outside their own cultural context, rather seeking to recreate their homeland on German geography. However, as I remind Germans who use that phrase, "If it is true that integration is a two-way street, then it is also true that the German side of the street is a three-lane autobahn and the migrant side is a dirt road." That is, there is an obvious power imbalance that gets covered up in such a saying. Migrants are forced to "be German" as much as they possibly can, every day of the week, especially if they are working or studying. It is understandable that migrants would seek out a congregation where they can be themselves and participate in the language of their souls. Along with the power imbalance, all too often the German understanding of "integration" is really more an expectation that migrants will assimilate and "become" German as much as possible, even though they can never really be German enough to escape all suspicion.[61] Expectations of assimilation, whatever word one may use for them, undercut even the simplistic understanding of a "two-way street."

Conclusion

The migrant experience is one of geographical-spiritual dislocation. The German experience is more generally one of geographical-spiritual comfort. Into these two differing contexts the sacraments of baptism and Communion can help God's new reality break through. To some the new reality will speak with a language of prophetic critique. To others it will speak words of comfort. Who will hear which words is by no means up to us. Indeed, we all may hear both words of critique and words of comfort. In this way the new reality of God also offers the opportunity of a new geographical-spiritual

---

61 Göktürk, *Germany in Transit*, 213.

milieu for both migrant and German. One that challenges the cultures and identities that we both bring to the table.

An uprooted plant is fragile and vulnerable, but when replanted in new soil, it can flourish again, and flourish in a way that may never have been possible had the plant not been uprooted in the first place. Beyond that, the newly transplanted plant has the potential to benefit a new ecosystem. It can add to biodiversity and enrich the environment. After taking the first radical step of becoming the image that our baptism proclaims we are, the next step of further opening the invitation to the Table can ensure more good soil than one hundred well-intentioned projects. Such a process may take longer, even longer than we like, but it can ultimately assure that we properly live the new reality of God.

EXODUS AS RESISTANCE
The Plight of Emerging Adults within the Church

H. Eduardo Boussón

University Minister, Nebraska Wesleyan University

No quiere usted dejarme ser yo, salir de la niebla, vivir, vivir, vivir.

— Miguel de Unamuno, *Niebla*

For church leaders, particularly those who are charged to recruit, equip, and deploy emerging adults, the weight of the world seems to be on their shoulders. It appears that at every opportunity we are reminded that the Church is shrinking, that we need more people, that we need more young people, and if we fail to reach new young people the Church will die. The more experienced I become, the less anxious I feel about this type of prophecy, in part because my work with emerging adults has opened my eyes to the new possibilities that are arising within their ranks regarding the future of the Church. Not surprisingly, these visions do not align with the current structures of the Church. The Church needs to exercise nimbleness in its way of recruiting and deploying emerging adults, so that this preferred future of

---

[You are not allowing me to be me, to escape this fog of existence, to live, to live, to live.]

37

a Church full of emerging adults is more than just hope. Joel's prophecy is coming to fruition, but we need to believe God that God is giving visions to our young to lead the Church into a new Promised Land.

In the next few pages you will read about colonialism in the Church, particularly The United Methodist Church (UMC). To say that The UMC has programmed colonialism within its structure is by no means a stretch of the imagination.[1] I have observed that the sentiment behind colonialism is alive and well in The UMC and our emerging adults are suffering from it. In response they are exiting the denomination as an act of resistance.

It is no secret that throughout history the Church has been used as an arm of colonialism, through its religious practices which imposed the language, practices, and worldview of a foreign power. Missionaries, perhaps unintentionally, instilled an understanding in the minds of the colonized that the foreign culture under which the Church operated was superior. This act of cultural violence was done in the name of the gospel. This constitutes spiritual colonialism.[2]

On Colonialism

A young man sat near the banks of a river, observing with great care the hustling and bustling around him. This was his home but he felt his heart was far away. The whole scene filled him with excitement, yet from time to time he would be overcome with sadness for what he had lost. He belonged to two worlds, one filled with metropolitan energy and the other marked by forceful displacement.

He had come to this riverbank, as he had many times before, to read. Reading was a way in which he kept alive the traditions of his people. On his

---

1   For a different treatment on this topic, see Robin Zape-tah-hol-ah Minthorn's chapter in this book on Native American young adults within The United Methodist Church.

2   This term is not new and is often used in the context of foreign religious missions. For the purpose of this paper, I would like to define it as the systematic use of foreign religious practices in order to erase or discredit a native expression of religiosity.

lap rested a new book that was just published. It was the story of a young man, like him, who faced the harshest of circumstances in a foreign land. This book had become a best seller. As he read the first page, the name of the hero, a man named Daniel, reminded him of another character from literature who was a defender of widows and orphans.

He read and identified with the adventures of this young man, who, like himself, was forced to leave his home, forced to bear a new name, forced to wear different clothing, forced to speak a new tongue. Still within this oppressive system, this young man created a culture of resistance. He refused to eat the food of the oppressor. He refused to connect with God in the style of the oppressor. He refused to live the life that the majority culture expected of him. After several hours of reading under a crisp Persian sun, the young man closed the book inspired to live a singular life that did not conform to the rules of the Persian Empire.

This story, though fictional, represents the plight of colonized peoples. The Jewish diaspora that occurred after 587 BCE created a body of religious books (Daniel, Esther, portions of Psalms) whose relevancy gives insight to the current treatment of youth and emerging adults[3] within the Church. These stories help us identify the system under which our emerging adults are being confronted within the Church. These stories help us see the exodus of emerging adults from our churches as an act of resistance.

As we turn to the biblical text of Daniel, we see not only a perplexing book but one with great social critique. It presents the complexities of living under colonial rule with insights into resistance. In it we see "slavery [as] the demise of symbolic institutions, name changes, hair or clothing, body markers, anything that symbolizes the death of one's identity and the birth of a new one given by authorities."[4] Daniel's character experienced these

---

3   I use "emerging adults" and "young adults" interchangeably. It refers to the age range of eighteen to twenty-six years. My experience is with emerging adults who are within a college setting.

4   Daniel L. Smith-Christopher, *Daniel: The New Interpreter's Bible*, vol. VII (Nashville, TN: Abingdon Press, 1994), 31.

while the author of the book sought to paint a faithful picture of the cultural intricacies of the Jewish diaspora. The story of Daniel is a story of Jewish courage as they faced the force of an empire.[5]

Even though authors today write books focused on slavery, I make the argument that colonialism has the same effects on subjugated individuals and their culture. Rephrasing their argument, colonialism is the removal of one's identity. When I address colonialism and the role of the Church in it, I also refer to my experience as a Latin American. Born and raised in Puerto Rico, I am part of a long history of colonialism and colonialism's religious expression. The late Uruguayan journalist Eduardo Galeano wrote that the conquering of the Americas came as an extension of the medieval mentality of the Crusades. I can remember as a young child seeing paintings of the Spanish ships who made the first encounter, their sails decorated with a red cross, the same emblem the crusaders carried on their shields. After all, "the expansion of the kingdom of Castile extended God's reign over the earth."[6] The expansion of the Spanish crown into the Americas had the same intent and desired outcome as the Crusades—the expansion of power, influence, and wealth.

This expansion, however, came at the expense of the natives who suffered from the greed of Europeans. There were dissenting voices such as that of Friar Bartolomé de Las Casas, who tirelessly worked for the fair treatment of the native people. He saw that it was not a desire to expand the kingdom of God but rather greed that promoted the conquest of the American continents. He writes:

> The reason the Christians have murdered on such a vast scale and killed anyone and everyone in their way is purely and simply greed. They have set out to line their pockets with gold and to amass private fortunes as quickly as possible so that they can then assume a status quite at odds with that into which they were born.

---

5   Smith-Christopher, *Daniel*, 31.

6   Eduardo Galeano, *Open Veins of Latin America: Five Centuries of the Pillage of a Continent* (New York: Monthly Review Press, 1997), 12.

Their insatiable greed and overweening ambition know no bounds; the land is fertile and rich, the inhabitants simple, forbearing and submissive.[7]

Because of the outcry of people like Las Casas, the Spanish crown created rules under which the conquistadors were to engage the natives. By the sixteenth century there was a law, *El Requerimiento*, that military captains were required to read to the indigenous people before any military engagement. This statement explained that if the listener did not adhere to the Christian faith, they would be dealt violence, their families enslaved, and their property taken away.[8] There was, however, no condition for a translator to be present. These examples and the history of the colonization of the Americas by Europeans present colonialism at its worst—a system in which the people of Africa; Asia; Oceania; and in North, Central, and South America have suffered the most in the last five hundred years.

Of course, colonialism did not end in 1898 with the fall of the Spanish Empire to the United States. It simply changed names. With structures already in place, United States continued its own influence in Latin America just as the Spanish did. Instead of overt political power, the United States exerted economic power to subvert political changes. As an example, we could point to the 1970s and the toppling of the Allende government in Chile, which was followed by the Pinochet regime. Even though this government was more oppressive, its procapitalist approach was more in line with the policies of the United States.

The case of colonialism in Puerto Rico, under the rule of Spain, followed by the United States, has been studied in depth elsewhere.[9] After the Spanish-American War, Puerto Rico became a colony of the United States. Being closer to the mainland than any of its other territories, Puerto

---

7 Bartolomé de Las Casas, *Brevisima relación de la distrucció de las Indias* (1552). English trans. of preface, "A Short Account of the Destruction of the Indias," accessed Aug. 1, 2016, http://www.columbia .edu/~daviss/work/files/presentations/casshort/casshort_13.html.

8 Galeano, *Open Veins of Latin America*, 13.

9 My favorite treatment of Puerto Rico's history comes from Fernando Picó's *History of Puerto Rico: A Panorama of Its People* (Princeton, NJ: Markus Wiener Publishers, 2006).

Rico became a fertile ground for rich crops such as coffee and sugarcane for the United States. By 1950, Puerto Rico's agriculture was mostly a single crop industry, meeting US sugarcane needs. Agriculture and its single crop economy was a way in which Puerto Ricans lived into their colonial status under a new nation. In March 1917, the US Congress granted citizenship to all Puerto Ricans. A month later the United States declared war on Germany, and eighteen thousand troops from Puerto Rico went to war. Via colonialism the United States mined Puerto Rican land for crops and people to serve in the armed services. It was vital for the United States to maintain the low level of education of Puerto Ricans so they would be funneled into the sugarcane fields or the military. About fifteen years ago during a family gathering in Puerto Rico, I remember asking an aunt (a professor at the state university) why she thought there were almost no public libraries in Puerto Rico. Her response was simple, "Because the Americans did not want an educated labor force in Puerto Rico."

The Church also played a role in this second colonization of Puerto Rico. Initially, Protestant churches were set up on the island to provide for the needs of government workers who had been appointed by the president of the United States. Puerto Rico became part of the United States in 1898, and the first Episcopal Methodist Church was founded in 1899.

The growth of the Protestant church in Puerto Rico came soon after. Island-wide evangelization promoted among Puerto Ricans a desire to join an institution perceived to be part of the United States. The first hymns were sung in English. The structure under which churches ruled themselves was democratic. These were new elements added to the Puerto Rican culture. Puerto Ricans had a closer experience of democracy by going to church. Puerto Rican adults learned their first songs in English from going to church. Boards of missions established schools and orphanages. These concerted efforts promoted a new culture. Other institutions would contribute to the colonization effort but the Church took the front seat. Currently it is estimated that between 30 to 40 percent of Puerto Ricans are Protestant.

When the desire for power, either seeking to gain or retain it, pairs with religious devotion, a union is formed where one justifies the other, so "we exercise power to advance religious beliefs" and "our power is justified by our religious beliefs." Even today the Church needs to be reminded and cautioned. When we exercise power over another human being, we are effectively dislocating them from the body of Christ.[10] Christianity is not about exercising power over the other but about sharing power through love. Jesus said that much when he said, "You shall love your neighbor as yourself."

I will not claim that the Church purposefully embraces this same philosophy today. Many things have changed since the 1970s, and one of those things is the Church's understanding of its role in the world. I would be missing the mark by stating that the Church understands itself or allows itself to be used as an instrument for power. That does not mean that the Church does not use its power to dominate minority groups. I believe and have seen that the Church still uses a structure that was built during an era of national expansion and colonialism. This structure mirrors the colonial system, and it subjects minority populations within the Church to it. This argument could be used about the displacement of ethnic populations, women, differently abled, and Gender and Sexual Minorities (GSM) people from the centers of power within the Church. I am arguing that this same type of displacement is occurring with youth and emerging adults.

On Emerging Adults

One favorite aspect of working in a university setting is the opportunity to sit down with students, staff, and faculty and visit. Usually the initial contact is mine. I send an email asking the person if she or he would like to visit over a cup of coffee or lunch, always my treat.

Some time ago I had the blessing of sitting down with Marie (not her real name). I was intrigued by this young woman's story. I had met Marie during her sophomore year. At that time I was advising a student organization that focused on service. Monthly, we would go out into the community

---

10 I enjoyed Timothy S. Moore's presentation, "Out of Joint," during the Colloquium on Displaced Persons, Cambridge, UK, July 18–22, 2016. See his chapter by the same name for other expressions of what it means to be dislocated from the body of Christ.

and spend a morning doing some type of volunteer work. Marie had that same drive to serve others.

What intrigued me the most about Marie was her experience of spirituality. She was passionate about the needs of others. I understand that many people are, but Marie was not just passionate; she also reached out in care and compassion. She was purely motivated by love. Theologically, I saw her behavior as a response to a religious experience. Yet, she never spoke of spirituality or religion. I was curious as to why she had such passion for others.

We started with small talk and moved into deeper conversation. I said, "Tell me about your spirituality." She looked down, somewhat puzzled by the question, and asked, "What do you mean?" I responded, "You know, what is your religious background?" Relieved by a clearer question, Marie went on to explain she was raised Roman Catholic but that she did not consider herself a Christian. She went on to explain all the things that she loved about Christianity: Jesus and his emphasis on love and concern for others, God's unrelenting love for humans and creation, and the idea of community.

"So, you believe in God?" I asked. "Yes," she answered. "And you believe in Jesus as God's son?" She replied, "Yes." I was genuinely puzzled at this time. "But you don't consider yourself a Christian?" Marie smiled, then continued, "I disagree with positions that my church has taken. I disagree with positions that Christians take. There are some things from other religions that I really like and practice. Plus, I don't think I know enough about the Christian faith for me to make a commitment. This is why I don't consider myself a Christian."

Marie is not unique in her experience of God. This transition away from childhood faith has been studied much over the years. As early as 1981, James Fowler[11] attempted to establish that, just as there are stages for psychosocial, cognitive, and moral development,[12] there also must be stages

---

11 James W. Fowler, *Stages of Faith: The Psychology of Human Development and the Quest for Meaning* (San Francisco: Harper & Row, 1981).

12 Jean Piaget proposed the stages of psychosocial development; Erik Erikson the stages of cognitive development; and Lawrence Kohlberg the stages of moral development.

for faith development. Using as point of origin Daniel Levinson's *Eras of the Life Cycle*, Fowler did not want to create an "achievement scale" or goals for people to hurry through. Instead he wanted to document the experiences that lead to different stages in the life of faith.[13] These stages represent where an individual should be at certain points in her or his life regarding faith development. His ideal stage for emerging adulthood corresponds to the fourth (out of six) stage, which he calls Individuative-Reflective faith.

During this stage, the individual is both emotionally and geographically separated from his or her place of origin. This separation drives an individual "to look with critical awareness at the assumptive system of values he and his family had shared."[14] In addition to the distance between the individual and the individual's previous system of values, there must also be "an interruption of reliance on external sources of authority."[15]

Other studies echo Fowler's claims. Jesse Smith argues for a similar process in adults who abandon theism. He explains this process in four stages: (1) being brought up in a religious (or somewhat religious) environment; (2) leaving that environment for one that questions theism by *unlearning* theistic beliefs and practice; (3) becoming atheist not as a rejection of theism but as a new identity; and, (4) coming out as atheist. What I found fascinating about this study is that this movement happens in the years of emerging adulthood. Young adults, like Marie, go to college, where they often question many of the assumptions of their childhood. Smith notes that "research has found that going off to college tends to be an important stage in individuals' lives in terms of experimenting with, and developing new identities and establishing a more autonomous sense of self."[16] This experience not only accomplishes an "interruption" with the individual's traditional sources of authority but also removes the individual from the emotional and geographical

---

13 Fowler, *Stages of Faith*, 114.

14 Fowler, 177.

15 Fowler, 179.

16 J. M. Smith, "Becoming an Atheist in America: Constructing Identity and Meaning from the Rejection of Theism," *Sociology of Religion* 72, no. 2 (2010): 223.

ties of her or his place of origin. It is crucial for the reader to understand that this study is about identity building and not about atheism in itself. Anyone would be missing the point by making the assumption that every individual who goes through this process will end up leaving theism. What his study reveals is what Fowler suggests. Emerging adults have encountered themselves in a position where they have to make choices regarding their beliefs to make sense of the world they live in. Marie is in that place. She is rejecting the practices of her childhood while fusing them with newfound meaning-making practices. This has led Marie to a currently emerging but more authentic and helpful religious identity.

Marie is not alone. Students are relying on new knowledge to patch holes or substitute aspects of their religious system. There are times when they completely substitute their beliefs in a similar process to what Smith proposes. In my experience, the vast majority of students do not go to that length. They find patches from other religious traditions to make meaning out of their experience of God. In many of my conversations, it is not rare to meet a Wesleyan Atheist or a Catholic Non-Denominational. These are students who have found doctrines from different spiritualties useful for their religious experience. Some of these doctrines include: social holiness, sacraments, the role of reason in religious thought, and the role of women in the Church and in social change. We cannot expect emerging adults to have a static faith. When parts or the whole of a religious system does not fit the individual's worldview, they have ease of access to unlimited amounts of religious practices through the multiple circles they belong to. They tinker with their religious system until they find the right fit for them. This characteristic of emerging adults is a trait that cannot be ignored.

Until recently, generational studies have been the authority under which we in the Church have understood the people sitting in the pews of our churches. We have felt the responsibility to create different ministries for the so-called baby boomers and the Builders and the intriguing yet elusive Generation X. Church leaders have been conditioned to use generational studies as genealogies. We have been taught that there is an understanding of succession with every generation. In order to understand one, the previous has to be studied. The genealogical framework is key: just as it is important to understand the relationship between an individual and her parents and grandparents and so on, so it is the same with the understanding of generations. Even more, according to previous patterns we are able to predict the behaviors and experiences of future generations.[17] "The problem with this way of thinking comes when we want to make broader generalizations about historical events and social change."[18] Even when this approach may have served to understand previous generations such as the baby boomers, it does not seem to be as relevant to the current generations of emerging adults. Robert Wuthnow makes an argument that there is no decisive historical event that has marked this current generation of emerging adults like the Vietnam War for baby boomers or World War II for the Builders. There are some interconnections regarding behavior that a previous generation like boomers holds in common with the current generation of emerging adults, such as a desired emphasis on experience and an affinity for small groups. In order to fully be in partnership with emerging adults it would best serve us to look at the sustained trends that are defining their generation instead of comparing them to a previous age group.

The first thing to point out is that this generation of emerging adults is taking longer in reaching full adulthood. It is not rare to see emerging adults struggling through college trying to figure out what they are supposed to be in life. They go to college and study what they are passionate about, but that does not necessarily turn into a career. Often the months before graduation are the busiest for me as I visit with frustrated college seniors who do not know what their next step will be. Some of them put their careers on hold for a year or two as they embark on traveling, sometimes

---

17 See William Strauss and Neil Howe, *Generations: The History of America's Future, 1584 to 2069* (New York: Morrow, 1991). The subtitle asserts the ability to predict generational patterns seventy-eight years after the publication of the book.

18 Robert Wuthnow, *After the Baby Boomers: How Twenty- and Thirty-Somethings Are Shaping the Future of American Religion* (Princeton: Princeton University Press, 2007), 3.

volunteering through international or national programs, a venture known as a *gap year*.[19]

This uncertainty about a vocational/professional life often delays their joining social institutions that require commitment and establishing roots. These institutions include marriage, having children, and joining a faith community. This perceived delay makes sense. Earlier generations had a shorter life span. In 1900 life expectancy for men was 46.3 years and for women 48.3. In 1950 men's life expectancy was 65.6 years and for women 71.1. In the year 2000 life expectancy was 74.3 years for men and 79.7 years for women.[20] In one century life expectancy rose by nearly thirty years. It is no coincidence that persons have more time to spend in different areas of their psychosocial development because our lifetimes are longer. It is taking longer for emerging adults to become adults.

A second thing to consider is that emerging adults are also *tinkerers*. "A tinkerer puts together a life from whatever skills, ideas, and resources are readily at hand."[21] I believe tinkering is something that is characteristic of our time, due, in part, to the wide accessibility of information we have today. For us, tinkering is unavoidable. We may tinker with our thoughts and opinions on any given issue, because there is so much information available to help us make sense of the world. Religious thought is not immune to this. I remember when I was two years removed from seminary; I was appointed to a church as an associate pastor. That same year the senior pastor preached a sermon series on Christianity and the religions of the world. The purpose of the series was to look at other religions and see what we could glean from them to make us better Christians. For example, Islam could teach us about the importance of prayer; Buddhism about meditation; Judaism about charity, and so forth. In my mind, that series was tinkering with religious thought. Tinkering cannot be seen exclusively with a negative connotation.

---

19 "The Gap Year Experience: A Life-Changing Opportunity," Test Prep, accessed July 03, 2016, http://www.princetonreview.com/study-abroad/college-abroad/gap-year.

20 Wuthnow, *After the Baby Boomers*, 10.

21 Wuthnow, 13.

Tinkering is something that we can do now because of the ease of access to information. At times we tinker with our thoughts and practices to justify destructive behavior. But more often than not, we tinker to enrich our lives. "The key to understanding the life of a . . . tinkerer is uncertainty. The tinkerer's life is sufficiently uncertain that it is impossible to solve problems through predefined solutions. . . . Our world is filled with the kinds of uncertainty that make tinkering a necessity."[22]

Emerging adults are taking longer to develop into committed community members, and they tinker with their lives out of necessity. These two characteristics have challenged a Church that is graying and that wants to function with certainty.

And the Church

Yvette is a leader on campus. She is smart and gets things done. The student organizations that she belongs to have asked her to be either the treasurer or the president. She also laughs a lot. Yvette always has a smile on her face that is contagious to those who see her. Most of all, she is filled with hope. Ivette's hope is not wishful thinking. Ivette's hope is an eschatological type of hope, the type that knows that at the end God will triumph. Yvette also is quite involved in the religious life on campus. She was born and raised United Methodist and is proud of that heritage.

As part of her involvement and leadership development I asked her to preach during one of our chapel services. I did not know what to expect, but she was good. I was impressed, so I began to ask myself, "Is Yvette called to professional ministry?" I was diligent and began to ask her questions regarding vocation. I gave her more responsibilities that were pastoral in nature. She excelled at all.

When I approached her to tell her, "Yvette, I think God is calling you to be a pastor," she responded, "Oh, thank you Eduardo, but I don't think so, I just don't feel it." She continued, "I don't think I'm cut out to preach

---

22 Wuthnow, 14.

every Sunday, do pastoral care, lead meetings throughout the week, deal with conflict in a church. . . . I have thought about it before, but I'm very clear that is not my calling."

Yvette is not alone. In the last three years I have sat down with over twenty different students who either thought they had a call to ministry or in whom I saw the gifts for ministry. Nearly all of them had trouble committing to the traditional forms of ministry, in part, because of the uncertainty of their present thoughts and understandings of reality. Emerging adults find themselves in a period of theological fluidity. At this point in their lives they do not see their family's (and church family's) faith as theirs. They understand that relying on this source of certainty holds them back from independence.[23] Trying to find their calling while at the same time defining their religious identity is a difficult task.

Emerging adults like Yvette are rare in my experience. In fact, it is hard to find young adults who are serious and committed to their faith.[24] "Emerging adults are, on most sociological measures, clearly, the least religious adults in the United States today."[25] The majority of emerging adults struggle with being religious due to the fact that they do not see its significance other than teaching morals. Students are not able to see differences between religions, much less the difference between Christian denominations. It is common for me to hear the following statements in any given conversation on campus:

> "All religions are the same. They basically teach us to be good."
>
> "I don't think I can be United Methodist because I don't believe that the world was made in seven days."
>
> "When I was little, I was hurt by the church. It is a bunch of hypocrites."

---

23 Christian Smith and Patricia Snell, *Souls in Transition: The Religious and Spiritual Lives of Emerging Adults* (Oxford: Oxford University Press, 2009), 150.

24 Smith and Snell, *Souls in Transition*, 151.

25 Smith and Snell, 281.

"My United Methodist Church back home teaches the same things as the nondenominational church in town."

"I cannot be part of a religion that hates others."

Most of these students were born and raised in a United Methodist church. As I listen to them I ask myself, "What did we do to fail these students? Where were we when they had these questions early in life? Did we teach them that it was okay to ask questions? Did we teach them that the heart of religion is the love of God?" This is the missional context of the Church. Even when these trends are active in America and Europe, there is no sense in thinking that the spiritual reality of emerging adults is much different in other parts of the world.

So how is the Church responding? Such fluidity of thought and differences in experience are being countered by The UMC with an overly relaxed approach to Christian education within the Church and a rigid process for credentialing professional ministry. A strong Christian education program that includes an emphasis on youth is a vital tool that emerging adults need in this time of individuation and reflection. What I have observed is that those who attended strong or established church-based youth programs that have both a social and a religious component have a stronger foundation. Strong, church-based Christian education helps address the impulse of emerging adults to claim a faith different than their parents' religious preference. In my experience youth who have taken this step before leaving their community are more willing to explore a religious vocation.

It is noted that most emerging adults entering professional ministry make a decision to do so before leaving home for college.[26] Unfortunately, youth ministry has stopped being a priority in many of our churches. Many churches make a large push for children's ministry mostly to attract young families. By the time the children become confirmed, churches, particularly those with limited resources, seem to struggle to keep their youth involved.

---

26 Lovett H. Weems and Ann A. Michel, *The Crisis of Younger Clergy* (Nashville, TN: Abingdon Press, 2008), 38.

All the churches with which I have been involved as a pastor, attendee, or consultant lament their frustration with Sunday morning sports, work, or other conflicting commitments. Parents seem to be content with the moral foundation that churches provide and more willing to provide opportunities for alternate skills once their children become youth. Confirmation is then viewed as a graduation of types from learning basic morals.[27] Perhaps this is viewed more clearly in regard to church school attendance. In twenty years (between 1985 and 2005) enrollment in church school for youth between the ages of fourteen and eighteen in The United Methodist Church dropped by 33.6 percent.[28]

Of those who have responded to full-time religious service, which in this argument are the ones most likely to have had strong religious instruction and the ones most likely to have claimed (or to have begun to claim) a distinctive religious identity, their number has dropped by nearly 250 percent in that same span.[29] "There is an urgent need for congregations to take more seriously the spiritual lives of young persons, to present them with a compelling theology, and to engage them meaningfully."[30]

The Church is displacing our young people. We have done this by substituting religious education with moral training. We have done this by seeing our children and youth as a way to attract younger families to grow our congregations. Unknowingly, we have objectified them as a means to an end. We have tried to mold our children and youth into something we feel comfortable with instead of shaping them into disciples of Jesus Christ. Through our system of Christian formation we have attempted to spiritually colonize our children and youth.

I believe that too often we are attempting to rein their identity and steer their religious development through the structures we have for recruitment

---

27 Smith and Snell, *Souls in Transition*, 149.

28 Weems and Michel, *Crisis of Younger Clergy*, 39. Enrollment in 1985 was 571,794 and in 2005 it was 380,476.

29 Weems and Michel, 476.

30 Weems and Michel, 41.

for professional ministry. In The United Methodist Church, each annual conference is given some freedom to tailor their process of ordination according to their needs. There are standards that every young person entering this process needs to meet. That said, each annual conference can ask more of their candidates, and some ask a lot more, causing the ordination process to take longer in some conferences than others. Regardless of these differences, the process requires of emerging adults things that might have been fair to ask in the past. Ignoring the emerging adults' current reality—their extended psychosocial development, process of commitment, and need for tinkering—contributes to their further displacement and their venture into less-structured religious traditions. Lovett Weems notes that some young clergy have experienced the ordination process as lengthy, perceiving it as hazing and as overly bureaucratic.[31] All these have the marks of a system that works to displace the identity of the current expression of emerging adults.

As I talk with students about religious vocation, they often respond they do not want to serve within The United Methodist Church. Their number one concern is, "I do not want to move every other year." Other concerns soon arise, including "I disagree with only pastors doing Communion," and "The Church will not accept my lifestyle." Listening to their concerns and learning of their fluidity, it becomes evident to me the mismatch that exists between The United Methodist Church culture and the culture of emerging adults.[32] Emerging adults are seeking religious meaning in smaller communities that are organic, often grouped by affinity. Even when it is difficult for me to keep count, on my college campus there are at least three of these communities that have formed in the last three years. They rent a house and live together. They also do Bible studies and worship in their own homes.

This is not new. Baby boomers did the same when they were merging into adulthood. I am not making a radical call to form house churches. What

---

31 Weems and Michel, 48.

32 Seeing a chart of the candidacy process compared to the reality of emerging adults makes me wonder, "What do they have to give up about themselves in order to be ordained?"

I want to call attention to is that emerging adults are exploring their faith; it is taking them longer; they are being more thorough, incorporating aspects of other traditions; and they are doing this organically. To listen to them and to be in partnership with them in this time of transition is essential for them to find a way back not as individuals who have to "pay their dues" and "conform" but as equals.

The Monkey and the Fish

A typhoon had temporarily stranded a monkey on an island. In a secure, protected place on the shore, while waiting for the raging waters to recede, he spotted a fish swimming against the current. It seemed obvious to the monkey that the fish was struggling and in need of assistance. Being of kind heart, the monkey resolved to help the fish. A tree precariously dangled over the very spot where the fish seemed to be struggling. At considerable risk to himself, the monkey moved far out on a limb, reached down, and snatched the fish from the threatening waters. Immediately scurrying back to the safety of his shelter, he carefully laid the fish on dry ground. For a few moments the fish showed excitement but soon settled into a peaceful rest. Joy and satisfaction swelled inside the monkey. He had successfully helped another creature.[33]

I love this story. As simple as it is, it conveys a great truth. It mirrors the historical missionary efforts of the Church. In his book on cross-cultural service, Duane Elmer makes the case that when we are doing missions we need to stop making decisions for those we serve. The Church must work together, in partnership, and not force expectations of what it seeks to accomplish. When it comes to missions and service, we have grown accustomed to offer a toxic charity, an approach to mission work that does more harm than good.[34] We need to adopt a missiology of liberation, one that seeks to

33 Duane Elmer, *Cross-Cultural Servanthood: Serving the World in Christlike Humility* (Downers Grove, IL: IVP Books, 2006).

34 I heard the term "toxic charity" first from Robert Lupton in his book of the same name (San Francisco: Harper One, 2012).

liberate one partner from a history of being dominated and the other from perpetuating domination.

Of course, this idea is not new. Paulo Freire calls the culture of domination "sectarianism." This is the culture that does not allow for independent thinking and that imposes ideas upon the other.[35] Instead, Freire suggests that for true liberation to take place, the process in which men and women are able to live free, a process of "radicalization" needs to emerge. Radicalization is the process through which the individual achieves and lives with a critical mind.[36] Sectarianism holds on to existing structures of domination. Radicalism frees the mind and the spirit to new possibilities. Freire states further that the liberation of the oppressed is also the liberation of the oppressor. In that process both become whole individuals. Freire's ideas have been with us for over forty-five years. I believe they have shaped the current view of missionary work in the church and the approach to volunteer work in secular society.

How do we become a beloved community with our emerging adults?[37] I believe we need to have a serious plan for the day when they begin their confirmation. Begin to listen to their voices then and there. Make them partners in ministry. Do not relegate them to take care of the nursery. Teach them and let them teach you what it means to be a leader today. Empower their critical consciousness. Make space for them to think critically about their faith. Teach them to think critically about their faith. It will be scary. It will be risky. Think of this biblical example: if Job had not thought critically about God, he would not have had the experience of the Divine that he had. When we teach our youth to think critically of their faith we are inviting them to deconstruct the ideas and concepts they have learned from their church and family. It is risky but I would rather have them experience this at home while under our care than miles away with complete strangers.

---

35 Paulo Freire, *Pedagogy of the Oppressed* (New York: Seabury Press, 1970), 31.

36 Freire, *Pedagogy of the Oppressed*, 21.

37 For a beautiful treatment of this question see Jeanne Roe Smith's chapter in this volume.

I remember vividly a youth retreat that my church would send me to every year. This was a conference youth event that we all eagerly waited for. On my first year I remember one of the preachers telling us that this was the time for us to know God. It was imperative for us to know God personally and not to worship the God of our parents. After all, the preacher said, God only has children, not grandchildren. I was fifteen at the time. I am grateful for this experience as it gave me permission to begin the journey of finding my religious identity. We need to make spaces for emerging adults to find their religious voice before going off to college. We do this by taking risks, helping them think critically about their faith, first by deconstructing it and then by providing spaces where they can build it again on their own terms. This process is a process of liberation.

As our emerging adults decide their vocations, we need to push ourselves and acknowledge nimbleness in our processes. I am not advocating for a reenvisioning of the candidacy process. My concern is that we are missing what God wants to do in the world when our emerging adults do not see a place for them in the rigidity of our processes. We need to come to terms with the fact that some of our emerging adults are called to be in ministry in ways we cannot begin to imagine. Our structure is limited by our imagination. God may be calling someone to ordained ministry within a coffee shop that offers a safe place for people to meet, with occasional worship opportunities. God may be calling some for ordination while running a neighborhood nonprofit, a pottery store, or a yoga center. We need to acknowledge that the Church is changing and that the Holy Spirit is stirring something new in the hearts of our emerging adults. We need to be nimble.

The work of the Church is not done. As we advocate in working with populations of different means than ours, we also need to adopt an attitude of working with emerging adults. My hope is that we have the vision to transform the systems in our church that objectify children, youth, and emerging adults, so we might work together with them, liberating each other, moving forward God's mission in the world.

Not long ago I was at an event in which a guest speaker was invited to reflect on her approach to creating a culture of calling within The United

Methodist Church. One of the main points was the ability of our annual conferences to bring young people into ministry. The speaker shared how these young people needed to be creative people who thought outside the box, people who were not afraid to take risks. The emphasis was that this is the type of pastor we need for the future of The United Methodist Church. As she spoke a brief discomfort began to grow within me, because I know people who are creative, who think outside the box, who are not afraid to fail, but the Church has not changed to make a space for them. Often we think of individuals who will be the next John Wesley and save The United Methodist Church, but we forget the scores of unknown individuals who worked with Wesley side-by-side to create a system in which they were liberated for service in the world. Our system needs to be nimble for what God wants to do in the world through them.

Robert Wuthnow is often asked if there is hope for the Church. "My view is," he replies, "that congregations can survive, but only if religious leaders roll up their sleeves and pay considerably more attention to young adults than they have been."[38] Listening and working together will create a new reality where they will be welcomed as equals. The journey that we have taken needs both a driver and a navigator, and the Church needs to take turns with the emerging adults at navigating and driving.

One of my favorite works of literature is *Niebla*, by Miguel de Unamuno. It tells the story of a man, Augusto Perez, who has lost his way. As he considers options, he decides to contact Unamuno himself for advice. In an interaction that is reminiscent of a scene from the Book of Job, Augusto realizes that he is a character in a novel by Unamuno, in which many issues are discussed including self-determination. At the height of the argument, Augusto proclaims the words in the epigraph at the beginning of this chapter, which, translated, mean: "You are not allowing me to be me, to escape this fog of existence, to live, to live, to live. . . ."[39]

It is up to us to reject any remnants of the objectifying colonialism that

---

38 Wuthnow, *After the Baby Boomers*, 230.

39 Miguel De Unamuno, *Niebla* (Madrid: Cátedra, 1994), 284. My translation.

has invaded every structure in the Church. This radical process of liberation may lead us into a new era where the Church not only works together with emerging adults but contributes to the emergence of a new Church where all individuals will be valued as equal partners in the work of God in the world.

THE BODY OF A LITTLE BOY

Matthew W. Charlton

Research Associate with Wesley House, Cambridge, England,
and Adjunct Professor, College of Theology and Christian
Ministry at Belmont University, Nashville, Tennessee

Two-year-old Aylan's tiny body was found washed up on a Turkish beach. He drowned after the boat he and his family were fleeing in capsized. The boat was overloaded with refugees from the Syrian civil war because so many desperately *needed* to escape the daily horrors of bombings, killings, kidnappings, and mortal deprivation. Aylan's father, Abdullah, was unable to save him. Abdullah was also unable to save his wife, Rahan, and his other son, Galip. This family was displaced, war refugees upon whom the international community makes a moral claim of care but practically does very little to exercise that morality.[1]

In many cases, a refugee must "arrive" first before care is extended. The journey in order to arrive, however, is the deadliest part. Thus, families, young children, mothers, and fathers die in the sea, or die from overexposure, or are kidnapped and sold into sex slavery, or experience all kinds of horrors that are inflicted on displaced persons. I remember seeing a picture of Aylan on shore, seeing most clearly the shoes on his feet. If you can bear it, find that picture

---

1 This is known as "the responsibility to protect," often shortened to R2P. For a brief description, see David Hollenbach, SJ, ed., *Driven from Home: Protecting the Rights of Forced Migrants* (Washington, DC: Georgetown UP, 2010), 8.

and look at those shoes. Those were good shoes that fit his feet, shoes that had been lovingly fastened so they would not fall off and be lost. I can see Aylan's mother and father putting those shoes on his feet, making sure they were snug, but not too tight, then looking up into his face and saying something like, "Is that OK? Not too tight? These are some good-looking shoes!" and then touching his little face lovingly. I can see this because I do this with my own children, making sure they are all squared away before sending them off to school, always telling them that I love them. That is what I see in that picture, the harsh reality that allows children to die because of politics, that allows families to be decimated due to war, and yet, signs of love abound in a world of decay. Abdullah spoke plaintively after losing his family: "I don't want anything else from this world. . . . Everything I was dreaming of is gone. I want to bury my children and sit beside them until I die."[2] One day, I would like to meet Abdullah, tell him I am sorry that the world we share is such a painful place, and then sit with him, weeping over the dead, the lost dreams. I believe I know where I can find him.

There is another familiar story. It is the story of the child Jesus. The Gospels tell of his birth and call gently to mind the Christmas season, full of sweet noels, candy canes, and Santa Claus. But the real story is much more disordered and chaotic, much more like the terror of Abdullah's family than the peaceful Nativity with which we have made ourselves familiar. Following the rather odd sequence of events that led to Mary's pregnancy, Joseph's consternation about Mary's possible infidelity, and the subsequent birth of Jesus, Joseph learned it had been ordered that the boy Jesus be killed. His parents, prescient to the danger, effected an escape, traveling during the night through dangerous and foreign lands to arrive at a place that was not their home, the land of Egypt. The boy survived, but the king in his rage and fear ordered the mass murder of all little boys.[3] The small family lived

---

2   "Syrian Toddler's Dad: 'Everything I Was Dreaming of Is Gone,'" CNN, Sep. 3, 2015, http://www.cnn .com/2015/09/03/europe/migration-crisis-aylan-kurdi-turkey-canada/index.html.

3   This we call "The Suffering of the Innocents." A horrid depiction of this can be seen in the South African movie *Son of Man*.

abroad, strangers in a strange land, until they were able to return, yet again not to home due to the tyranny of a new king, but to Nazareth, in Galilee. Jesus and his parents, Joseph and Mary, survived while untold numbers of others did not. According to the scriptures Joseph, like Abdullah after him, was faithful in seeking to protect his small family from the ravages of a dangerous world. Although not much is heard from Joseph after the opening scenes of the Gospels, I can see him also lovingly fastening the shoes on Jesus's feet, touching his face with a tender look of bottomless love and care.

These are the stories of two children, their families, and the homes that were too dangerous to hold them. Two thousand years separate them and yet they are similar. The same threat of death is a reality for untold numbers of girls and boys, mothers and fathers. The dilemma of migrants and refugees has not shifted. The human race has made little improvement in our ability to face displaced persons with compassion, a lack rooted in the refugee's absolute need and the suspicion that accompanies their strangeness. In the name of safety and security, the displaced person is displaced again and again, forced to live an existence that is an ongoing plunge into uncertainty, constant fear, and early death.

In the opening years of the twenty-first century, thousands of children have been killed in the Syrian civil war while millions have fled their homes and towns, from Kunduz to Damascus to South Sudan. The volume of refugees and migrants is massive, and receiving nations are having practical and political difficulty managing the arrivals, who often end up in camps and settlements grudgingly managed by host countries,[4] if they are received at all.[5] The kind of refugee a person is matters—internal or external, economically

---

4 An article by Lauren Collins in the February 27, 2017, edition of *The New Yorker* describes the particular struggles of unaccompanied minors. Collins notes that nearly thirteen thousand of the refugees seeking asylum in Europe in 2015 were unaccompanied children under the age of fourteen. Additionally, she notes that "more than ten thousand migrant and refugee children have gone missing in Europe since 2014." In this moral crisis, the human community's ability to care for the youngest and most vulnerable is glaringly deficient (52–61).

5 At the time of this writing, the Republican regime in Washington, DC, is seeking to forbid refugee resettlement in the United States for those who are displaced from certain countries, in particular Syria, for which a six-month freeze is proposed. Efforts are also underway to diminish the number of legal immigrants.

or politically persecuted, victim of climate change or natural disaster, or some combination thereof. The United Nations High Commissioner on Refugees (UNHCR) estimates that more than sixty-five million people are currently forcibly "displaced."[6] This word describes any person who is uprooted from home and community for reasons beyond their control: war, climate change, drought, threats of death due to religious affiliation, threats of death due to sexual orientation, gang violence, civil war, lack of food, loss of family stability, loss of a job. The factors that contribute to displacement are various but the result is the same. A person or a family must leave a place they know as home, become strangers in a strange land.

The church has a complicated relationship with compassionate hospitality and especially with the care of the alien, stranger, sojourner, foreigner, refugee, immigrant, the ones who are perceived as the most threatening by the host culture because they look different and sound different. Emigres may not understand the system of religion and social codes that organize a community. They might have a system of religion and social codes that are more compelling and upend the receiving community's sense of stability. In the Hebrew scriptures, care for the foreigner was an absolute command, because the people of Israel were once strangers in a foreign land. The law codes of the Torah are replete with commands to not "wrong or oppress a resident alien" (Exod 22:21). "When an alien resides with you in your land, you shall not oppress the alien. The alien who resides with you shall be to you as the citizen among you; you shall love the alien as yourself, for you were aliens in the land of Egypt: I am the LORD your God" (Lev 19:33-34). The prophets, too, weighed in. "Thus says the LORD: Act with justice and

---

6   The principle source for this data is the United Nations High Commissioner for Refugees (UNHCR) at www.unhcr.org. As of June 2017, this is the summary from UNHCR: "We are now witnessing the highest levels of displacement on record. An unprecedented 65.6 million people around the world have been forced from home. Among them are nearly 22.5 million refugees, over half of whom are under the age of 18. There are also 10 million stateless people who have been denied a nationality and access to basic rights such as education, healthcare, employment and freedom of movement." Susan F. Martin offers a brief history of the formation of current efforts regarding refugees as well as providing a primer on the categories of refugees, detailing why these categories are important, limiting, and limited, in "Rethinking the International Refugee Regime in Light of Human Rights and the Global Common Good," in *Driven from Home*, ed. David Hollenbach.

righteousness, and deliver from the hand of the oppressor anyone who has been robbed. And do no wrong or violence to the alien, the orphan, and the widow, nor shed innocent blood in this place" (Jer 22:3).

It is also worth noting that the law and the prophets have some concerns with aliens presenting an affront to God, to the people, and the safety and security of Israel. For instance, there are multiple places where the law indicates there will be "one statute" for residents and aliens. Isaiah begins with a divine warning that "aliens devour your land," yet within the context of Israel not being faithful to the commands of God. For Israel, faithfulness requires a stance of justice and care toward those who are displaced from home. To oppress them, to treat them unfairly, is to not keep faith with the will of God. Conversely, for the foreigner to disobey the divine law is to invoke the judgement of God. In the end, the assumption is that God is one God and the people are one people, and there will be one law applicable to all given by the one God. And yet, the scriptures themselves, while testifying to the revealed God, are also the testimony of human disobedience and failures of care and compassion.

The church has long recognized the plight of the "stranger in a strange land." It is part of the church's shared history with Israel's exodus, exile, and diaspora. The Western tradition following Augustine has been that the church is itself merely passing through, struggling against sinfulness and corruption on its way to the Holy City. This view can lead to an ethic of disengagement, where the immediate concerns of the "world" are of less importance than the necessity to maintain a purity of faith. The story of Jesus is one of forced migration and itinerary, fleeing from danger and walking toward death. And yet, to follow in the way of Jesus is redemptive, and thus the church receives, welcomes, and aids those who are displaced. It is meritorious to receive the stranger. If the language of merit is anathema, then it is a moral imperative of those who follow Jesus to receive the stranger, for in such acts does one receive Jesus and the beloved of God: "Do not neglect to show hospitality to strangers, for by doing that some have entertained angels without knowing it" (Heb 13:2).

In the 2016 US presidential election, white Christian evangelical voters voted significantly as a group for a person whose platform included closing the borders to refugees, deporting immigrants, and building a wall to keep people out.[7] To be fair, white voters generally seemed to have backed these policies, but white evangelical Protestant voters support these policies and the person pushing them overwhelmingly. This group continues to hold these views, even as a majority of those polled in the United States do not back these immigration proposals.[8] The question this raises is: why do white evangelicals support policies regarding immigrants and refugees that seem to be directly opposed to the religious tradition of which they are a part? I am certain there are many reasons for this, with a concern for safety and security standing out. This concern is expressed as fears over Islamic extremism in the United States and in the world, a fear that, according to Pew, is broadly shared across multiple religious and racial groups.

Without a doubt, the life of a forced immigrant or refugee is not a desirable existence. The risks are extreme: lack of permanent shelter, insufficient and substandard food, lack of potable water, kidnapping into sex slavery, poor working conditions and low pay for those who are able to find work, and the advanced likelihood of an early death. As a colleague said to me some weeks ago, her husband's family put him as a young child on a boat from Vietnam, because the uncertainty of life at sea was better than the certainty of death at home. From Abdullah's family to the Holy Family, the overwhelming themes that play out in refugee and immigrant scenarios are the safety of home, the danger of home, the threat of homelessness, and the sense of death stalking. Even with the relatively unambiguous testimony of scripture regarding the "stranger," we see that "Bible believing" Christians lack an openness to those who must migrate. On the contrary, the migrant is seen as a threat. By no means are evangelical Christians in the United

7   G. Smith and J. Martínez, "How the Faithful Voted: A Preliminary 2016 Analysis," PRC, Nov. 9, 2016, http://www.pewresearch.org/fact-tank/2016/11/09/how-the-faithful-voted-a-preliminary-2016 -analysis/.

8   G. Smith, "Most White Evangelicals Approve of Trump Travel Prohibition," PRC, Feb. 27, 2017, http://www.pewresearch.org/fact-tank/2017/02/27/most-white-evangelicals-approve-of-trump-travel -prohibition-and-express-concerns-about-extremism/.

States the only group whose actions seem to contradict the teachings that prescribe care for the foreigner. Examples may be drawn from around the world. Xenophobia is in every place.

Would not the human race help each other in seeking the safety and security of home for every person? I know I would rather be home in my community than become a near-permanent resident of a refugee camp. I would rather my children grow up in safety and in a strong community, with good schools, plentiful food, close friends, and known, trustworthy adults and mentors. With the state of the world in 2017 as it appears to be, the valuing of home, community, family, and the peace of the state is diminished and has completely deteriorated in some places like Syria, parts of Somali, and with particular dangers to minority ethnic communities such as the Rohingya people in Myanmar. Millions of people are on the move, fleeing from home to anywhere, nowhere. The world's ability to help appears to be exhausted, and scapegoating the migrant as a criminal, terrorist, or someone looking for a handout with no state loyalty has risen in equal measure.

In the absence of the political will and the perceived practical ability to meet the vast needs of migrants and refugees, the church and people of faith and goodwill must be engaged in providing for the needs of those without a home, who now live in hope of the hospitality of strangers. The people of God are called and commanded to show hospitality to strangers, to foreigners—the responsibility of care is ours. Christians are a people of faith, hope, and love, anticipating the Kingdom of God by participating in the Kingdom of God, through our shared love of God and neighbor. William O'Neill writes that our actions in this regard are "no mere supererogatory act of 'charity.' Hospitality is the measure of righteousness, our token of belonging."[9] In a very real sense, the Christian tradition understands hospitality as the offer of home to those who are guests, strangers, and victims. The Greek word translated as "hospitality" is *philoxenia*, possessing nearly the exact opposite

---

9   William O'Neill, "The Place of Displacement: Ethics of Migration in the United States," in *Living With(out) Borders: Catholic Theological Ethics on the Migrations of Peoples*, ed. Agnes M. Brazal and María Teresa Dávila (Maryknoll, NY: Orbis, 2016), 70.

sense of *xenophobia*. The Wesleyan tradition would view the practice and embodiment of hospitality as an act of mercy and means of grace as an effect of God's grace at work and a sign of growth in spiritual maturity.

To practice hospitality as no mere charity but as crucial to one's faith is to live more fully into the grace given by a God who clearly identifies with and seeks to protect the migrant. God has a preferential option for the poor, of whom migrants and refugees are clearly those in the most dire need. Yet, as Gutiérrez notes, God's preferential option for the poor also includes those who suffer from a spiritual poverty submitting to the will of God for God's people, which must include caring for the poor and the immigrant.[10] The poor, the immigrant, and the refugee have needs that may be met through the spiritual abundance of God's people. But, as noted above, there are many who claim to be God's people who suffer from an intense spiritual poverty that causes them to see division as unity, hate as love, scapegoating as care and compassion, and the stranger as the enemy.

It is difficult to separate faith from politics, even more so when either or both become ideologically entrenched. An American conservative evangelical may truly believe that his or her faith requires some form of care of the refugee but will interpret that through a political ideological lens. To be fair, progressives do the same thing in different ways. However, the testimony of scripture is not ambiguous on the care of the stranger. God, and God's people, identify with and are migrants, refugees, strangers in a strange land. As a reminder that this is a real experience and no mere abstraction, Agbonkhianmeghe E. Orobator writes: "God migrates and God moves out of a distant or remote existence of divinity toward human history, not in an abstract manner, but in a concrete, palpable experience of establishing a dwelling in time and space. The theological rapprochement suggested in this imagery of a displaced, mobile, or migrant God reinforces the ethical

---

10 A short description of this point may be found in the introduction to the revised edition of Gustavo Gutiérrez, *A Theology of Liberation: History, Politics, and Salvation,* 15th ed. (Maryknoll, NY: Orbis, 1988), xxv.

imperatives of hospitality, refuge, finding home and protection for the displaced and migrant peoples."[11]

Since I started working on this short chapter some time ago there have been thousands more like Aylan, thousands more children like Jesus, thousands more families like Abdullah's and Joseph's fleeing political and economic turmoil. One result of this increase in refugees and immigrants has been the rise of racist nationalist and populist groups. Another result has been the rise of voices speaking out on behalf of immigrants, refugees, and other powerless and homeless people, many of whom are people of faith—Christian, Muslim, Jewish—and countless others of goodwill. Remembering the advice of Nancy Bedford to make little moves against destructiveness, my family has taken on what we can to advocate for and support immigrants and refugees. We have had Sudanese and Somali refugees at our home to share a meal. We have protested racist groups and racist ideologies and have communicated with our elected representatives, convinced that, as a society, we can offer care and compassion to those who are displaced. My heart breaks thinking of the thousands more children that will die, families that will be torn apart, and homes and homelands that will be destroyed on behalf of prideful gain and despotic power. The Christian faith with which I am most familiar calls the people of God who claim Jesus Christ as Savior to rise up against such demonic forces as human beings are capable of, working always to transform hearts and minds through the grace of God and the love of Jesus Christ, whose resurrection continues to show the power of love and familial care over the temptations of death and destruction.

---

11 "Justice for the Displaced: The Challenge of a Christian Understanding," in Driven from Home, ed. Hollenbach, 41.

PITCHING AND MAINTAINING A TENT OF HOSPITALITY FOR DISPLACED PERSONS ON CAMPUS

Amy L. Fisher

University Chaplain, Suffolk University, and Denominational Counselor to Methodist Students, Harvard Divinity School

YHWH appeared to Abraham by the oak grove of Mamre while Abraham sat at the entrance to his tent in the heat of the day. Looking up Abraham saw three travelers standing nearby. When he saw them, Abraham ran from the entrance of the tent to greet them and, bowing to the ground, said, "If I have found favor in your eyes, please do not pass by our tent. Let some water be brought, that you may bathe your feet, and then rest yourselves beneath this tree. As you have come to your faithful one, let me bring you a little food, that you may refresh yourselves. Afterward you may go on your way." "Very well," they replied, "do as you have said." Abraham hurried into the tent to Sarah and said, "Quick—take a bushel of fine flour and kneed it into loaves of bread." Abraham then ran to the herd, selected a choice and tender calf, and sent a worker hurrying to prepare it. Then Abraham took cheese and milk and the calf which had been prepared, and placed it before the travelers; and he waited on them under the tree while they ate. (Gen 18:1-8, ILV)

* * *

A young couple were feeling very crowded in their small house, and they went to the Rabbi to ask for advice. They expected to hear how to make their house bigger. Instead they were told to invite relatives to live with them in their small house. They complained to the Rabbi that this did not make the house feel bigger but rather even smaller! The Rabbi unexpectedly told them to bring their farm animals and all their pets inside as well. Each time they returned to the Rabbi to complain, the Rabbi told them to bring more living things inside the house. When they could take it no longer, the Rabbi said to them to let all the relatives, farm animals, and pets leave their small house. Suddenly, the house seemed much bigger for just the two of them, albeit less interesting. (My adaptation of a traditional Jewish folktale from Poland.)

* * *

An Interfaith Center may be likened to a tent, a tent of hospitality for all and a place of mutual inconvenience for all. Pitching one is both inconvenient and often impractical. Have you ever set up a tenting site in a campground only to have vandals knock it over? Have we not all picked a bad site? The soil is too barren. The river is too far away. All the good sites were already taken.

As difficult as it is to pitch a good tent—especially for novices—it is even more difficult to live inside. It is too small. It is too cramped. We cannot sit or stand or eat as we might normally. But for our survival we must learn to both pitch the tent and dwell inside.

Different religions on college campuses must learn to coexist, not merely apply a bumper sticker label to a problem but name a proposed solution: an Interfaith Center. The challenge for those in the Methodist/Wesleyan tradition is to succeed in extending the right hand of "fellow"ship when it is the most inconvenient. We may enjoy the solitude of our siloed offices and grand foundations, but when we find ourselves sitting alone it is time to open the doors and unshutter the windows and see who is waiting outside. And we must admit why they feel unwelcome.

Before suggesting what an Interfaith Center should look like on our campuses, we must catalog who is "on the outside." Then we need to look at ways to pitch the tent and set up an Interfaith Center as well as look at how we maintain the tent on a daily basis. Finally, I believe this is not a mere theological exercise but is critical to the survival of the Methodist/ Wesleyan tradition.

The perfect specimen of Methodist piety is the one who is most convenient to entertain with our familiar camp stories and fireside chats. While they may no longer exist, they might be the first to approach our tent of meeting. Or they might be the ones we think we see, and we may greet them to find they have other relevant spiritual questions that are inconvenient. Who else is disenfranchised and waiting to be invited in to the table?

Who Is Waiting to Come In?

One day while I was occupied in organizing religious volunteers in the Interfaith Center, a female student knocked on my open door. After inviting her in and engaging her in conversation, I learned that she needed a job. Another office had told her to go see the chaplain—me. She explained to me that she was a refugee from Serbia and had come to college for a better life. She had first been supported and encouraged by the local Jewish Vocational Services (JVS). This day, however, she had trekked from campus office to campus office looking for employment.

Asking her what she thought she could contribute to the Interfaith Center, she replied, "You need more religious opportunities for Serbian Orthodox students!" She was right. They were waiting to come in to the Interfaith Center. And she knew how to welcome them.

Over the next few weeks she invited members of our university community to her Serbian Orthodox festivals and services. She reached out to welcome the stranger. Before she left the Interfaith Center on the day I met her and at the end of our conversation, she said to me, "By the way I am tired and hungry to help, and I going to remain sitting in this chair until you let me help." She was not going to leave unless I hired her. I did. She got her own desk and chair at the table of hospitality.

Soon afterward, a student from the Rainbow Alliance organization on campus asked me to prepare a program for his upcoming meeting. I agreed and asked him what the topic would be. He replied, "Can you explain to us why God hates us? We figured that since your tradition discriminates against the Gender and Sexual Minorities [GSM] community you would know." Meetings ensued, and I was able to guide the Rainbow Alliance through textual interpretations of the Sodom and Gomorrah story, 1 Corinthians 6, and Romans 1 in the New Testament. Entertaining their questions with honesty and integrity made them more welcome in the tent.

Marginalized Muslims are making up an increasingly greater component of campus life. Ignorance of the Qur'an and ignorance of differences between Islamic groups make all persons poorer. A Muslim student seeing an icon of Mary behind my computer desk exclaimed one day, "I am so glad to see that you realize Mary wears the hijab just like me. I feel welcome!"

Religious "nones" are everywhere, and they may not come into our religious life offices; yet they take Religious Studies academic courses. A religious none once asked me, "Why should I believe in an unjust God? Look what's happening in the world! How could a just God not make all the marginalization stop?" You know others on your campus whom you have not welcomed: Pagans, Indigenous persons, anti-theists, Jews, and on and on.

If we open up to all, it is going to get crowded in the tent. How can we live this way? How can we not? Inconveniently, none of these may want to be Methodist or be part of the Wesleyan tradition. But they are able to enrich our already diverse congregations.

Pitching the Tent

Looking at the unwelcomed, what do we as college chaplains need to do to pitch a welcoming tent of inclusion for all? First, we need to check our language. Do women want to be called fellows? Does the Gender and Sexual Minorities (GSM) community want to be called homosexual? Labels hurt but using someone's preferred name can ease an open wound.

Second, we need to check our space. Do we have a large church with an old rugged cross on our campus? The easiest way to pitch an inclusive tent is to start from scratch, but most colleges and universities do not have that luxury. But what if you did have a blank canvas? There should be images on the walls that invite interpretation and inclusion. A graduating student's mother came by to see me one day. She wanted to give the Interfaith Center a gift that symbolized to her the way her son felt in the Interfaith Center as a participating student. She said to me that she hoped I liked it, but I should not feel obligated to display it. Her humility was inspiring. She unwrapped a package with a small square piece of wood. On it was an icon depicting Sarah and Abraham entertaining the strangers in their tent. She said, "My son arrived at the university a total stranger from Greece but he felt welcome in the Interfaith Center." I put the icon on the wall of the Interfaith Center and it has been there ever since. Another student from India thought the Interfaith Center should have a proper brass "Om," the sound that the universe makes in the Hindu tradition. This brass icon now hangs next to the icon of Abraham and Sarah and the welcomed strangers.

Third, an Interfaith Center need not be labeled "Chapel." A Muslim student told me that at his school the unwelcoming sign "Interfaith Chapel" was removed and replaced with the welcoming sign "Interfaith Center" and now he feels welcome.

Fourth, an Interfaith Center needs to have flexible space. Is there room for Buddhist meditation on the floor as well as Roman Catholic mass and Protestant praise and worship services? Are there texts from all the world's religions and objects from non–text-based religions? Are there places for all gender expressions and identities to make ablution and not just baptismal fonts? Are kosher and halal foods available? All these things will signal hospitality.

Maintaining the Tent

As in the Polish folktale, a crowded dwelling needs to be carefully thought out and organized. Theologically, equality, respect, and hospitality are key. When welcoming the stranger we must realize the stranger brings new experiences that do not always conform to old traditions. To continue to exist as a Christian denomination we must continue the dialogue with other denominations, other religions, and within The United Methodist Church.

Ask These Questions:

1. What is there to be afraid of?
2. What if the other is right; does that make me wrong?
3. Do I fear someone else may be better than me?
4. What if we are all just following different paths without the same goal?
5. What if the Methodist/Wesleyan tradition is not meant to be the dominant religion in the world?
6. What if dialogue with the other is all there is?

Next, Make the Schedule

Who gets priority in scheduling the tent? No one. Extend a logical flow of hospitality, and let each tradition set the table in their own way and invite others inside. If it is Friday night, set up a Shabbat dinner and open it to all who are hungry. If it is sunset during Ramadan, set up a halal breakfast and open it to all who are hungry. In other words, invite everyone to every service, program, Mass, or meeting, no matter how inconvenient. Be prepared to give an explanation for the event. Be prepared to be asked the hard questions, and be prepared to wrestle with your own honest answers. Bring everyone inside the tent.

A student asked me, "Why don't you lock the door after you finally leave at night? Is it because that would be inconvenient for those of us looking for a welcoming place even if no one is here to greet us?" Indeed, an overcrowded, inconvenient Interfaith Center should always be open and welcoming. Even when no one is watching.

If you are interested in starting an Interfaith Center or would like more information, you are welcome to contact me at interfaith@suffolk.edu and follow me on Twitter @RevAmyFisher.

Questions for Reflection

1. Describe your current religious life office. Who works there? Who uses it?

2. Who feels unwelcome in your religious life office? Why?

3. Who or what is in the way of making your religious life center welcoming to all students, staff, and faculty? Your administration? Your parish council? Your donors? You?

4. Who can help you envision a welcoming Interfaith Center?

5. How will you know that you have succeeded in pitching a welcoming tent?

For Further Reading

Inclusive Language Bible. New York: Rowan and Littlefield Publishers, 2007.

The Sublime Quran. Chicago: Kazi Publications, 2012.

REFLECTIONS ON WAR, POVERTY, HUNGER, AND DISPLACEMENT

Marta Landaverde Rodriguez

Pastor, Evangelical Methodist Church, El Salvador

O f late, we have started our mornings listening to news regarding persons who are subjected to mistreatment, to the point of losing their lives, in trying to reach another country. There are many stories that we might tell; and it seems a contradiction, because in spite of globalization and different nations' attempts to unify the world, we become more separated daily, given that the phobia against different cultures and some men's interest in being superior to others does not allow for understanding but instead fills us with resentment and makes us act in a violent manner.

In the following pages, three important points will be developed regarding war, poverty, hunger, and displacement. Given that, together, they provoke so much pain, it is worthwhile to study each one of them and the impact they have on our contexts, because in spite of not acknowledging the fact, these phenomena affect the entire world: some in different contexts, but they are ever-present realities. We will begin by conceptualizing each one and by touching upon some special points in outlining them, since the general concepts are within the reader's grasp. Next, we will discuss the kingdom of this century, which is obviously directed not by God but by human beings who, in doing everything for their own advantage, consciously or unconsciously ignore God's command regarding love. Believing themselves to be wise, they become foolish and deny the existence of God as a way to justify their decisions; and they call persons who profess faith ignorant and old-fashioned. In the presence of a world corrupted in its sin, we will end by recalling that, faced with so much pain, discrimination, and perversion, there is hope, because the Church of God, no matter what denomination, has been called to bear witness to the kingdom of God, in order to offer signs of hope; to announce good news of great joy, knowing that it is as yet a time of justice and redemption, that the promises of God in scripture are not a myth; neither are the words dead but living and effective. Sadly, the Church as well has become part of the world's problems: erroneous theologies that corrupt sound doctrine, producing leaders and pastors that only pastor themselves. Instead of fulfilling the mission that God has given us, they are enriching themselves and impoverishing their flocks (for example, the theology of prosperity, among others, which seeks the benefit of some by selling the blessings of God).

It is necessary for us to proclaim the true gospel, as Mortimer Arias has stated: the Gospel of the Kingdom,[1] because this is the real one, the one that Christ taught, a space where there is justice, restoration, and forgiveness.

I trust in God that you may have wisdom to read this chapter written from a Central American perspective in which I describe the reasons for displacement, so that you are unafraid to encounter persons from a different culture, for you do not know what they have experienced and what they are perhaps going through still.

Concepts That Are Known but Not Understood

We will begin with generally well-known concepts regarding the social problems in question, but we will contribute to a different understand-

---

1   See the prologue to Mortimer Arias, *Venga tu Reino, La memoria subversiva de Jesús* (Mexico City: Casa Unida de Publicaciones, 1980), 16.

ing from a Central American perspective as well as provide some statistics about their extent in our society, how they are related to each other in such a way that they always go hand in hand, and their alarming effects.

War

This term has many definitions, depending on the point of view in which we explain it, but it seems to me that the most coherent and simple definition is the one that the dictionary of the Royal Academy of Spanish Language gives: war is "struggle or combat, even in a moral sense." Now if we stop to think about this, we can conceive that war is a problem that begins in a moral sense and grows to the point of reaching a physical point, so that we may say that war does not begin with violent confrontations: everything begins in thought, which later gives way to expressions that harm the morale of others, and this leads to belligerent actions. In this sense, war is a process that reaches its climax in the use of violence of great magnitude, such as we experience today, those of us who listen to the statistics and are sometimes part of such numbers, but in the end we do not know whether these deaths matter or not, because a way to solve the disagreements is not sought. Nature itself is witness to the terrible atrocities that human beings have been capable of inflicting. We only have to recall events such as Hiroshima and Nagasaki, where not only were human lives lost but the ecosystem suffered deadly losses as well.

War is resorting to violence when ways to reach agreement regarding conflicting issues are not found; saddest of all, in the majority of cases the issues at play are economic interests, the reason for which countries quarrel among themselves, since money gives them power, and power gives them authority over the least, in order to exploit them even more. Thus, we may agree with the Apostle James when he writes:

> Those conflicts and disputes among you, where do they come from?
> Do they not come from your cravings that are at war within you? You
> want something and do not have it; so you commit murder. And you

covet something and cannot obtain it; so you engage in disputes and conflicts. You do not have, because you do not ask.[2]

If the powerful nations do not reach agreements that put an end to conflicts, war will continue to take the lives of innocent people, as we have recently seen in the wars in the Middle East, and the attacks perpetrated on civilians in the countries involved. Even if someone is in the military in a certain country, they are fighting for the ideals of others, and in most cases only benefiting those others and not the person carrying the weapon. It is worthwhile at this point to remember the words of Monsignor Romero to the Salvadoran Army, and to all those who carried weapons in that dark war that El Salvador lived through: "Brothers, you are from our own people, you kill your own peasant brothers and when you are faced with an order to kill given by a man, the law of God that says, 'Thou shall not kill,' must prevail."[3]

Many times we think of war as an item in a newspaper and we forget that it is a reality that many experience daily; one which strikes and causes pain; one in which speaking of the number of dead means that there are also many families crying for loved ones and burying them; a reality in which families sometimes do not even know where their loved ones' bodies are, and in which the uncertainty regarding the whereabouts of their missing family members pursues them their entire lives.

My country, El Salvador, is living through a silent war: violence between gangs and police inflamed by institutions steeped in corruption that hide the social reality from the world, fearing the withdrawal of foreign investment. The impact of this silent war is more evident with each passing day. This is a situation that cannot be ignored. Though this is not an openly declared war, last year the United Nations classified Salvadoran gangs as terrorist groups that permeate cities, assault and loot communities, and intimidate families, driving them out of their homes and stealing the innocence of our children and youth. It is a war between brothers, a war in which politics

---

2   Jas 4:1-2.

3   See the homily of March 23, 1980, *Día a Día con Monseñor Romero* (Madrid: PPC Editorial, n.d.).

mixes with drug trafficking and corruption; where the breakup of families, lack of values, and old war wounds become freshly opened in the face of poverty; one in which we are once again waiting for a miracle of salvation for our land. This is the reason why many of us understand that war is not a choice; violence generates more violence: an eye for an eye is no longer an option. Jesus calls us to love our enemy; thus we can say that it is a time for agreement and not repression; where the well-being of the people must prevail and not the petty interests of groups that benefit in the midst of problems.

Poverty

We may understand poverty as a lack of resources necessary for human survival, but in a fuller sense the resources that make a person poor are not only material but also moral and spiritual. We normally relate poverty to a lack of food, housing, and health services, among other things; but this lack is the result of the depreciation of moral and spiritual values that humanity suffers. The contrast between rich and poor is more and more extensive. It seems incredible to know that half of the world's wealth is found in the hands of only sixty-two persons, and the rest of the wealth is equally disproportionate, since according to a report by OXFAM,[4] 1 percent of the world's population possesses more wealth than the rest of the world; this should make us reflect on inequality and on those men and women affected by unemployment or by armed conflict or natural catastrophes. Sometimes we think that it would be so simple to solve the problem of poverty if only we could bring them health and knowledge; if only those who have so much would share their wealth with those who have not; if only unjust taxes did not have to be paid; if only the world stopped living in inequalities caused by ill-gotten wealth, life would be different; if only we allowed for the commandment that Christ gave us to

---

4   Oxfam International, "62 personas poseen la misma riqueza que la mitad de la población mundial," Jan. 15, 2016, www.oxfam.org/es/sala-de-prensa/notas-de-prensa/2016-01-18/62-personas-poseen-la -misma-riqueza-que-la-mitad-de-la.

be fulfilled, the one that says: "You shall love your neighbor as yourself."[5]

There are global statistics that offer data on the reduction of extreme poverty, but we must also remember that this is due to the opening of some services that governments place at the disposal of their citizens, that in theory, at least, benefit the most vulnerable areas of developing countries; this does not mean that the people already have all that they need; because sometimes they are technically trained in some trade, but there are no job opportunities; other times, there may be a hospital near the communities, but it is out of medicines.

I also want to discuss a truly harmful kind of poverty: sinful poverty.[6] This is poverty in which people are capable of doing anything for a few crumbs of bread but also in which the rich person, in order to maintain status, exploits, marginalizes, hurts, steals, and kills. This person, desperate to satisfy his or her desires, is blind to the human being who is capable of selling his soul in order to gain what he wants. Love and mercy vanish before us and we do nothing; we feel powerless in spite of the fact that we are bearers of hope; we see the world collapse and do nothing. We cannot continue to be only spectators of the pain of others, or of our own pain, either; we must find a way to contribute to changing this reality.

I should also mention the ethical poverty of those who are elected by the citizens to serve the people and who end up serving themselves from the contributions and taxes of the workers. They become parasites of impoverished societies, and instead of improving the conditions of their communities they end up exploiting God's poor.

In Deuteronomy 15:7, God sends his people some practical rules regarding poverty: "If anyone is poor among your fellow Israelites in any of the towns of the land the LORD your God is giving you, do not be hardhearted or tightfisted toward them" (NIV). Selfishness blocks the way for us to be able to share the blessings that God gives to human beings; that is the reason

---

5   Matt 22:39.

6   Monsignor Oscar Arnulfo Romero, "La Iglesia de la verdadera independencia, la Iglesia de la auténtica libertad," sermon, Sep. 11, 1977, El Salvador.

for inhuman justification for the existence of poor people in the world, such as: "There are poor people because they are lazy and don't want to work"; "people don't work because they don't want to." We see work as the only way to get out of poverty, but it does not only require work, because many people work but for such a low salary they are exploited to the point of exhaustion, and they receive salaries that are laughable and unjust. Also, in the majority of cases there are no job opportunities. El Salvador has one of the highest rates of unemployment in Central America; one out of four young people are out of work.[7] This is an alarming and telling statistic, since unemployment is one of the reasons that young people join gangs or migrate to other countries in search of new opportunities.

No matter what category, poverty speaks to us about the struggle of men and women to survive and be able to bring the necessary sustenance to their families. As we consider this, we can say that we have many poor in the world, given that wealth is concentrated in very few hands and there are many who do not have what is necessary to live in dignity. It must be mentioned that the poor are a manifestation of the injustice known as Poverty, this being the sin of those who accumulate selfish profits. On the other hand, being poor is not a shameful circumstance, since in our need or weakness we can experience the salvation and strength of our good God. The Apostle Paul tells us in Philippians: "I know what it is to have little, and I know what it is to have plenty. In any and all circumstances I have learned the secret of being well-fed and of going hungry, of having plenty and of being in need. I can do all things through him who strengthens me."[8]

But neither can we be silent before the advance of this world scourge; we need to make the effort necessary to alleviate this situation, an effort in which not only are world or national leaders involved in seeking alternatives for change but one in which all humanity should be involved. "Greater still

---

7   Central America Data.com, "El Salvador: Formal Employment Continues to Decline," Sep. 7, 2017, https://www.centralamericadata.com/en/article/home/El_Salvador_Formal_Employment_Continues_to_Decline.

8   Phil 4:12-13.

should be the contribution of the Church as a light of hope in the midst of darkness and as the voice of those who have no voice,"[9] not only by denouncing but by creating development programs for the most vulnerable in our communities and in the entire world, according to our abilities, truly becoming the hands and feet of God in this world.

God did not create poverty; when we talk about "God's poor," we are talking about the preferential option of God for the poor and not about the existence of poverty. For this reason I can say that poverty is the result of the pride, selfishness, and violence of human beings against themselves, who out of a thirst for power oppress and exploit others. In this sense, we understand that poverty does not exist in the purposes of God for his creation, since everything that "God made was good."[10]

There are many factors that lead to poverty, but no matter the reason for it, God looks with compassion upon the poor and needy in such a way that, understanding their condition of fragility in the world, God responds to their cry: "Then the LORD said, 'I have observed the misery of my people,'"[11] and this is not only due to the lack of food but also the lack of those who, though wealthy, recognize their need for God in their lives, such as Cornelius, the devout centurion to whom Peter was sent to share the good news,[12] who, in spite of his economic status and not being a Jew, was a man who feared and sought God.

God does not accept persons on account of their economic status; God's preference for the poor does not mean excluding the rich from the plan of salvation but rather emphasizes responsibility for the goods accumulated in their power, and toward their less-favored brothers and sisters:

> If there is amongst you someone who is in need in one of your cities,
> in the land that the LORD your God has given you, do not harden your

---

9 *La voz de los sin voz: la palabra viva de Monseñor Romero* (San Salvador: UCA Editores, 2007).

10 Gen 1:31.

11 Exod 3:7.

12 Acts 10.

heart nor close your hand against your brother in need, but rather open your hand liberally.[13]

This is a call to share the economic blessings that God gives us: not only to the rich and powerful but also to those of us who may not have a lot—the little we do have, we should not hesitate to share.

Finally, I want to discuss one more category: the poor in spirit. These are the ones who recognize their condition as "dust"[14] and who need God in their lives as much as they need air, water, and food, and who tirelessly seek God for this reason. The poor in spirit are those who heed the call of their Shepherd because they recognize his voice and obey him; they are those who know that they are only stewards of the riches of the Owner of gold and silver, and they will give an account one day before the Owner and Lord of all for everything laid in their hands. For this reason, the kingdom of Heaven is reserved for them. This is poverty that we must seek, for it will keep us closer to our heavenly Father; it will direct our steps in such a way that we will love the Lord our God with all our mind, with all our strength, with all that we are; and we will love our neighbor as ourselves.

Hunger

This is the term used to express the need for food in the human body. Food intake is a necessary action for a person's existence; the lack of food is a cause of illnesses and even death. The world today has diverse practices resulting in forms of hunger. Some, by choice, vow to stop eating for a certain period; others go hungry due to physical, mental, and spiritual illnesses. Dieting, fasting, and the lack of eating due to temporary illness cannot be equated with true hunger. There is a kind of hunger that is not a choice, which is unavoidable: hunger brought on by a lack of food due to natural causes (such as drought, floods, plagues, etc.), which leads to food scarcity throughout the world. The damages from global warming are rapidly approaching the

---

13 Deut 15:7-8.

14 Eccl 12:7.

point at which they will be irreversible. We must be ecologically aware and work together to protect what we have left.

Also unavoidable is hunger caused by economic policies that benefit rich minorities and increasingly subjugate the impoverished majority, who are left without the power to purchase basic necessities such as food for their families. This type of hunger is cruel, since it depends on abusive and arrogant governments that declare themselves in austerity for social investment but which spend state resources lavishly, such as in celebrations and unnecessary travel, and so forth. This is the type of hunger that is the fruit of social injustice, a growing need. Statistics show us that approximately 795 million people in the world do not have enough food to lead healthy and active lives. An effective work force is required, but no mention is made of the workers' diet: the majority of them eat neither breakfast nor lunch, because the money they have is used for transportation and to support the children left at home. How will the expected work performance be achieved, if the workers suffer from malnutrition or die of hunger?

Poor performance in school and dropout rates must also be analyzed from another perspective and not only from a psychological and sociological point of view, since often the children, both adolescent and young, leave school in order to work and bring home bread. In the case of women, they are often criticized for selling their own bodies or staying with abusive spouses who mistreat and humiliate them for the sole purpose of ensuring bread for their children and a bit for themselves. The humiliations to which they are submitted are well known: they receive no training, no resources, no essential education for a healthy life. Even sadder is the fact that without opportunities in life, hunger submerges them in such a world of degradation that they find themselves capable of doing anything for a piece of bread, anything to survive.

Talking about hunger from a perspective of examining statistics is easy, since from a distance we may observe a "social phenomenon"; what is sad is to be part of a statistic: feeling hunger in one's own flesh, going to bed with an empty stomach, seeing your children beg you for food and having nothing to give them; wanting to nurse your baby with breasts dry due to malnutrition.

How can a father or mother remain silent when their children's stomachs are rumbling with hunger? The people cry out for justice, and the hunger of the poor does not go unpunished:

> The cry of the Israelites has now come to me; I have also seen how the Egyptians oppress them. So come, I will send you to Pharaoh to bring my people, the Israelites, out of Egypt." But Moses said to God, "Who am I that I should go to Pharaoh, and bring the Israelites out of Egypt?"[15]

Hunger exists because of the gluttony of others, and hunger is not only for food but for justice. For this reason we say that hunger for food is the most visible indicator of the atrocities that are being committed in a nation; but much more lies behind: there is repression, marginalization, discrimination, and death. The most frustrating thing is that no one answers for those who are suffering; the world becomes unjust; under the cover of national sovereignty or the free will of the people, they turn a deaf ear to national issues; and although we have laws that protect our rights, very few are willing to go against the system and seek justice.

We see political leaders, judges, and prosecutors taking years to make their judgments, trying to hide the truth that is openly known. El Salvador knows, through the voice of the people in the midst of war, who killed the Jesuit priests, who assassinated Monsignor Romero, but the trials are still ongoing, trying to determine who is responsible; these are truths that are known but not recognized. Because of hiding the truth, hunger and thirst for justice grow because pain does not heal. Jesus said, "Blessed are those who hunger and thirst for righteousness, for they shall be filled."[16] Human justice takes time; and often it does not arrive; it becomes adulterated; it makes mistakes, but God promises us that in him, we will find true justice.

---

15 Exod 3:9-11.

16 Matt 5:6.

Displacement

Displacement means to "move from one place to another," which is commonly associated with migration but is not the same thing, since to be displaced differs in the following:

⊕ Displacement is moving from one place to another forcibly due to a sudden natural disaster (floods, earthquakes, among others); armed conflicts (wars); violence (death threats, mistreatment).

⊕ Displacement is carried out in collective movements and is not the decision of a single individual but rather of the community; moving for the purpose of providing safety for the group but with the clear intention of returning to the place of origin.

⊕ Displacement can be both internal and external. It is internal when the families or communities move within their own national territory; for example, in the case of armed conflict, communities move to neutral or less-affected areas. In cases of natural disasters, people move to places of lower risk. But there is also external displacement, when a group is forced to cross borders seeking safety. Such is the case of refugees who seek asylum due to the imminent danger in which they find themselves, and to which receiving countries must respond, and the response is many times uncertain, since they are not always well received: refugees are seen as a danger, as intruders. We live in two-faced societies, speaking of how poorly people live in other countries and that we must be humanitarians, but when it is time to put our ideals into action, we change our minds and question the presence of strangers among us. Nations sign treaties of cooperation as well as many pacts that offer protection and assistance to persons affected by displacements, but many times they deny asylum, which often is no more than an excuse, because fear is behind such a denial—fear of that which is different.

Displacement is a palliative solution to an emergency; given the circumstances the people affected are experiencing, it causes severe psychological, and sometimes physical, traumas. For this reason they ought to receive better attention on the part of the entities involved and from society in general. Because displaced persons are snatched from their homes, they leave everything: their lifelong employment, their history, their essence as a person, in order to move to an unknown place where they will find new customs and where everything will be different. During the years of El Salvador's armed conflict, I lived in one of the areas that was least affected by the war. There I met families who came seeking refuge for their children, to protect them from being recruited in either of the warring bands or from being shot in open conflict. These families struggled to adapt to their new homes but they were unable to settle in; they rejected returning to their places of origin, even before the peace agreements were signed. But others had to leave the country and resettle in foreign locations due to political persecution and the imminent danger they and their families faced when they were accused of being guerrillas.

In some processes, asylum for refugees is given—all the conditions are favorable so that the displaced persons can move and go on with their lives, but this does not mean that they will be well received by their new neighbors. Unfortunately, in the world we still have racial prejudices that do not allow us to receive the foreigner well, and I say this in general, since saying that we are hospitable is easy; what is difficult is to practice it. In spite of being an ethical Christian value, hospitality is a challenge for all, since racial prejudice invades us and prevents us from being able to open ourselves to receive people without distinction. Since the Convention of Human Rights and the implementation of programs against discrimination and the punishment it carries, this continues to be an imminent scourge. Currently, in the Northern Triangle (Guatemala, Honduras, and El Salvador), one of the focus points is displacement of children and adolescents who travel to North America; in recent news it is evident that the main reason for their migration is to escape being recruited into gangs.[17] This problem not only promotes displacement abroad, but in our same small country, there is an unprecedented number of abandoned homes.

---

17 David Marroquin, El Salvador.com, "Mas Mil Niños [. . .]," June 17, 2016, http://www.elsalvador.com /noticias/nacional/191721/mas-de-47-mil-ninos-slavadorenos-detenidos-en=ee-uu/.

A recent study in the department of San Miguel, located in the eastern part of El Salvador, claims a total of two thousand homes have been abandoned due to the fear of besieging gangs, and where occupants have fled to find a safer place for their families.[18]

Displacement in the Northern Triangle of Central America is due precisely to the factors discussed above: war, poverty, and hunger, which provoke the flight of families or communities from their homes toward an unknown, and sometimes fatal, destination, such as the one experienced by three Central American children[19] who recently traveled to the United States and tragically drowned in their attempt to reach safety.

Displacement is not a new idea; since biblical times we are told about moments when Israelites were forced to move due to pressing circumstances. Thus, we should be prepared and aware that one day the displaced may be us. Therefore, we should remember that we are children of the same Father who created one world for all; that we all breathe the same air, that we all enjoy the same sun and water, and that we ought to share what we have with love.

The Kingdom of Human Beings

History is a faithful witness of these social phenomena: war, poverty, hunger, and displacement; these four continually walk hand in hand. During different times they present themselves in different conceptions and contexts, but in the end the consequences of these four are the same. And we see the detonating points in all wars; we find hunger and poverty at the bottom, this leads to war, which drives displacement. None of them are part of the creation of God; they all come from the sinful heart of human beings, who, blinded by the lust for power and wealth, do not care about the harm that they may do to their neighbor. Without measuring the consequences, governments go to war, forcing the most humble—those who do not even

---

18 El Salvador.com, "Dos Mil Viviendas [. . .]," July 27, 2016, http://www.eldiariodehoy.com/noticias/nacional/21692/dos-mil-viviendas-abandonadas-por-el-miedo-a-las-pandillas/.

19 El Salvador.com, "Mueren ahogados [. . .]," July 22, 2016, http://www.elsalvador.com/noticias/internacional/194580/mueren-ahogados-3-ninos-migrantes-en-rio-fronterizo-con-mexico/.

know the reasons for the disputes—to fight for "their nation"; justify wars for reasons of national pride, with their economic interests hiding under the table; and anyone who is against such a war is against the nation. This is to justify, in a simplistic manner, a war that will take invaluable lives. Since all of us are the creation of the blessed hands of God, every life lost is an irreparable loss, a terrible loss.

We Christians go throughout the world preaching the good news, saying that each life is worth the blood of Christ poured out on the cross at Calvary; but many of those who make the decisions to go to war call themselves Christians and risk the lives of their brothers. The world fights for power; someone wins and the one who does becomes a leader, and in the end the poor continue to be poor. A clear example of this are the soldiers themselves, who after their military service do not have many job options, and those who were wounded in the war struggle to survive, totally unprotected, because even health care is denied to them; and let us not talk about the hunger pensions they receive, if they are lucky. This is when we awaken from the nationalist dream and realize that we are only helping others to satisfy their lust for power.

The kingdom of human beings is unjust; it is a struggle for power without respite, where the one who has more money, more weapons, is the one who wins, forgetting completely that this world does not belong to us because we did not create it; we were placed here to be stewards of it, to protect it. The owner is the one who will call us to account one day; we have not done what we were committed to do: "The LORD God took the man and put him in the garden of Eden to till it and keep it."[20]

But humanity departed from the beginning, disobeying God, without realizing that he was rebelling against a being more powerful than he; no matter how many weapons human beings have, they cannot be compared to the power of God, since everything that exists has been made on the basis of what he created.

---

20 Gen 2:15.

Every day we see this world in decline: more people who do not believe in God; others who say they believe in God but never have time for him; others who take advantage of faith in order to enrich themselves; others who justify their actions by faith itself. We begin changing the word of God to suit us, making our own doctrines, submitting them to our own will, just to respond to the whims of our "members"; we surrender to ourselves, avoiding the word of God and what it says to us: that we cannot justify our bad actions. It is time to return, as the prophet said, to "the ancient paths,"[21] seeking the good way, because there we will find shelter for our souls.

Kingdom of God

> The Spirit of the Lord is upon me, because he has anointed me to preach good news to the poor. He has sent me to proclaim release to the captives and recovery of sight to the blind, to let the oppressed go free, to proclaim the year of the Lord's favour. . . . Today this scripture has been fulfilled in your hearing.[22]

The coming of Christ favors the establishment of a new order and the coming of a new kingdom that will bring hope to all. Many of us maintain that the *Imago Dei* was disfigured at the beginning of all time by sin, an image that with the coming of Christ begins to be reestablished, since the changes that originate not only affect people but have an impact on all creation.

In this sense, we understand that this new order is nothing more than the reestablishment of the original purpose of God for his creation. Now this new order has challenges to overcome; two thousand years ago a vision was given to us, as well as a renewed mission for our minds, and only those who accept this challenge have struggled and continue to struggle to fulfill it. When Jesus declares the changes that must take place once he has come, he promises a new kingdom for human beings, one that is different

---

21 Jer 6:16.

22 Luke 4:18-19, 21.

from those which men have formed, as demonstrated by history: a history of wars, death, hunger, destruction, lament, and pain. He offers assurance of a kingdom of hope, where the least shall be first, the forgotten will be exalted, and the vulnerable will have a defender. This becomes utopian at times, something unattainable that will never happen, but we forget that everything God promises, he fulfills. As Jesus said, "Today this scripture has been fulfilled in your hearing." This means that his Kingdom is here.

But as we see evil persists in the world—injustice, hunger, social problems—it can be difficult to believe his kingdom is here. How is the kingdom of God present, if there is so much pain? Why do hunger, poverty, war, and displacement increase? Two thousand years after the announcement of a new kingdom in this world, things continue to get worse instead of better; even the cross that announced the forgiveness of sins and was the sign of this new kingdom of love was used as a justification for war. Now, it is necessary to understand that this new kingdom is not of this world, and that is the reason why human beings continue to do their own will and why evil continues among us. Jesus did not come to impose his kingdom; he came to invite people to be a part of it, where everyone submits to his will, which is written in Holy Scripture. No one becomes part of this kingdom by force; neither is anyone forced to remain outside of it; it is a personal decision, which also implies that weaknesses exist in this Kingdom, because it is made up of human beings, and sometimes we get away from the will of God and from God's purposes, in order to fulfill our own.

"Church is the space where the Holy Spirit manifests the will of God to the world";[23] thus, it is expected that the kingdom of God become evident through the church. This is the reason that many affirm that the Church is a Sacrament, a visible sign of the grace of God, but sometimes the reality is very far from this.

Now, the *Parousia* of Christ made evident the errors committed by the people of Israel, in their attempt to be the "chosen people of God." If we

---

23 Pablo Andiñac, *Ser Iglesia*, 1st ed. (Buenos Aires: Lumen 2007), 17.

reflect upon this, the Church has also fallen: we have forgotten the poor and we despise the stranger.

There are times when we may see a church that has gotten away from its purpose: a church concerned with improving its infrastructure, increasing the number of its members, having a better theology, having better music. It is not bad for us to be concerned with these things, but we must also bring alongside the ministry of love that Christ has taught us. The Lord Jesus walked with his people; ate with those who were in the streets, cried with his friends; affirmed women; gave hope to children and denounced the injustice of the priestly order at that time, who had turned the House of the Lord into a den of thieves. For this reason, it is vitally important that we consider whether the Church of today is following the steps of Jesus: since we have been called to be his disciples, it is his steps that we must follow.

Recently I met a young student who came to spend the summer in El Salvador to learn Spanish and to get to know the cultural context of the area. One of the most challenging moments for this person was having to preach on the lectionary reading for the day (Luke 12:1-21). This person said to me, "How will I preach on this passage? How will I tell these persons not to accumulate wealth and to guard their hearts from greed? How will I tell them not to worry? They have nothing, and no matter how much they work, they never have what they need for their homes. I cannot preach this." It was a beautiful moment: that someone could understand this reality, since it is one thing to see the numbers of undocumented or displaced persons, and another to know why they are in their situation—what they are fleeing from, why they risk so much.

Nowadays, there are many books and articles that talk about the "preferential option for the poor," but it causes pain and sadness to see how little this is put into practice. We can fill a thousand books and talk about this for years, but if we do not act it is for nothing. I want to share the witness of John Wesley and his experience in going to seek the poor, not only as part of his Sunday preaching in the church but as part of his life of communion.

> Friday and Saturday I visited as many poor as I could. I found some of them in their underground cells, others in their attics, half of them

suffering hunger and cold, along with weakness and pain. But I did not find anyone unemployed who was able to drag themselves across the room. The common argument, "they are poor because they are lazy," is so evil and diabolically false. If you were to see this with your own eyes, could you spend money on ornaments and superfluous things?[24]

This statement also reminds us of what the Apostle James had previously recommended to us: "And if a brother or sister is ill-clad and in lack of daily food, and one of you says to them, 'Go in peace, be warmed and filled,' without giving them the things needed for the body, what does it profit?"[25]

One of the great problems we encounter is the lack of contact we have with people; we cannot speak or write about what we do not know; you cannot explain hunger if you have not experienced it. We cannot help this decadent world unless we leave the temples and walk with poor children, youth, women, men, and aged persons. We can make manifestos, declarations, and public protests about our disagreement with the policies of our governments, which we understand is part of the prophetic action of the Church, but it does nothing for us if, upon returning to our community, we are enemies of our neighbors or mistreat the people who work for us: we have definitely become resounding cymbals, but without the love of God in our hearts. We will make a difference when we fill our whole life with the love of Christ, placed in favor of our brother or sister, while conscious that each time we do good to one of the least of our brothers, we serve Jesus.

I met a woman who long had worried about her minor children, as they were constantly at risk of being recruited by the gangs of El Salvador. With great pain in her heart she encouraged them, as an only alternative, to migrate north, hoping it would save them from violence and destruction. With tears in her eyes, she accepted being separated from them and gave them all she had (which was not much) to assist them on their journey, with

---

24 John Wesley, *The Journal of John Wesley* (Chicago: Tyndale, 1951). Entry for February 8, 1753.

25 Jas 2:16.

the sole intention of preserving their lives, even though it meant she would never see them again.

Many times we have a simplistic vision of those who leave their countries. For many, the American dream loses its charm the moment in which the lives of their children fall into danger, and they have no option but to flee. It is not for dollars that they look abroad, but for a way in which to save the lives of their children. The migration of children has been widely criticized and managed inadequately by the countries involved, but the base has very complex structural problems. The solution must come from the hearts of human beings who urgently seek God and are led by his love toward providing relief and resolution. This is why it is painful when the displaced person is only seen as a stranger in a foreign land, who comes to "steal" jobs, who actually performs the worst jobs for an unfair wage, who is often seen as a delinquent who threatens the life of communities, without being given the opportunity to be known and accompanied on their life journey. In truth the displaced are potentially angels who have come to live near.

The church has the prophetic call to denounce injustice, but it also has a pastoral calling; these callings are not directed at the pastors, deacons, or leaders of the Church, but to each one of the members that make up the congregations: if you denounce an injustice, be careful that you are not unjust; take care you are not lying; and if you talk of walking beside the poor and marginalized, I hope with all my heart that you are doing something for him. We cannot be talking of love and supporting war; one single fountain cannot give two types of water: either it will be sweet or bitter; our lives must bear witness to the spirit whose we are.[26]

Let us be careful not to become philosophers of Christianity, or as John Wesley would say, not be "half Christians," because we are the Church; we are ambassadors of that Kingdom so longed for by the world. The church acts not only on Sunday in the temple, it acts every day and in all places where we go. We are the Church, called to give glimpses of hope in this world, in

---

26 Rom 8:14.

order to relieve hunger and poverty, and we will do it by sharing what we have; whether we possess a lot or a little, we must share. We are called to stop war and love our neighbor; this implies learning to be tolerant in the face of the differences we have; it implies not having a higher opinion of ourselves than what we ought to have,[27] where pride and vain glory are replaced by the humility that Jesus Christ showed us. Perhaps we cannot stop displacement, due to the circumstances of the world, but neither is there a reason to give up and not do anything.

It is worth highlighting the efforts of the Methodist Churches in the United States, Mexico, and Central America, which together with Global Ministries and the National Plan for Hispanic Ministry started a project called "Pastoral Accompaniment Along the Migrant Route."[28] The Church should not sit idly by: we can pray, knowing that our prayers are heard by our heavenly Father; but we can also join existing projects and efforts or create new ones to offer support to these, our brothers and sisters. We should remember that we are called to be holy as our God is holy, and that there is no holiness but social holiness, as Wesley said so well: "The Gospel of Christ knows no other religion but social religion, no other holiness but social holiness."[29] Therefore, if we call ourselves Christians, we must act like Christ and strive to bear the fruit that as his followers it is necessary to have.

We cannot say we love God if we are not in solidarity with those who suffer, if we continue to serve this world rather than the least of the kingdom of God. We are messengers of hope and this world needs us right now; let us not turn a deaf ear to this situation; let us respond from wherever we are, involving ourselves in the cause of Christ. Let us leap out of our comfort to save a life; that life—and God—will thank you for it!

---

27 Rom 12:3.

28 Felipe de Jesús Ruiz Aguilar, Hispanic UMC, "Cuidado Pastoral [. . .]," May 29, 2015, hispanic.umc. org/news/cuidado-pastoral-a-lo-largo-de-la-ruta-con-migrantes.

29 *Works* by Wesley, Volume IX, 39–40.

BEING DISPLACED ON YOUR OWN HOMELANDS

The Narratives of Native American
Young Adults Finding Space in
The United Methodist Church

Robin "Zape-tah-hol-ah" Minthorn

Assistant Professor, University of New Mexico

Introduction and Background

ative Americans[1] continue to have high attrition rates that begin in high school and continue throughout college. In 2005, statistics revealed that less than 50 percent of Native American high school students graduate. Historically, Native Americans have had high drop-out rates and low graduation rates.[2] Thus, Native Americans who make it through high

---

1   The interchangeable word use of Native American, Indigenous, and Indian will be used in this chapter. The preference of terms should be asked of each Native American person rather than assuming one term is sufficient for all.

2   Susan C. Faircloth, John W. Tippeconnic, and University of California, Los Angeles, Civil Rights Project / Proyecto Derechos Civiles, *The Dropout/Graduation Crisis among American Indian and Alaska Native Students: Failure to Respond Places the Future of Native Peoples at Risk*, 2010. Catherine Freeman, Mary Ann Fox, and National Center for Education Statistics, *Status and Trends in the Education of American Indians and Alaska Natives* (Washington, DC: National Center for Education Statistics, US Dept. of Education, Institute of Education Sciences, 2005), http://purl.access.gpo.gov/GPO/LPS91065.

school and continue on to college find out that they are few and far between. Although the latest report from the US Department of Education (2005)[3] shows that enrollment for Native American college students has more than doubled over the past twenty-five years, Native Americans remain under-represented in higher education.[4]

This background information provides context for the general Native American college student population. When we look more closely at the rates of Native American college students in non-Native colleges and universities (NNCUs) and then those in United Methodist–affiliated institutions and seminaries those numbers dramatically decrease. To explore the relationship of Christianity, spirituality, and access to programs specifically within The United Methodist Church (UMC) for Native American college students and young adults as they navigate their respective higher education journeys and life experiences, I conducted a study.[5] The goal was to help the church understand its influence on the access and programs and to help frame the historical narrative of missionary work, assimilation through Christianity, and contact between Europeans and Native American tribal nations. This chapter reports the results. The study used a mixed-methods approach with former and current young adult United Methodist Native Americans and those who have had exposure to various UMC-related programs to better understand their lived experiences and provide a deeper understanding of the context of culture and identity and its acknowledgment.

The survey was sent out to various former and current young adult United Methodist Native Americans about their use of UMC-related programs with

---

3   Freeman, Fox, and National Center for Education Statistics, *Status and Trends*.

4   Heather J. Shotton, Shelly C. Lowe, and Stephanie J. Waterman, *Beyond the Asterisk: Understanding Native Students in Higher Education* (Sterling, Virginia: Stylus, 2013).

5   This study was approved by the University of New Mexico IRB process as exempt and received support from the Oklahoma Indian Missionary Conference superintendent. The recommended names were provided by the OIMC superintendent and initial recruitment e-mail was sent to invite them to participate with the study through a link to SurveyMonkey. There is no identifiable information to connect the quotations to respondents. I would like to thank the OIMC for their support of this project and the Native American young adults who shared their experiences and recommendations.

the hope of having at least twenty participant responses. The use of both qualitative and quantitative surveys allows for a deeper understanding of the lived experiences of Native American young adults in their experiences of UMC-related programs in connection to their culture, identity, and specific spiritual traditional practices to their Christianity. The hope is that this study and the voices of the participants will highlight their lived experiences, while providing suggestions for ways to improve UMC-related programs to honor and support Native American young adults who are displaced within their own homelands.

Section I: History and Context

Christianity, Missionaries, and The United Methodist Church

Prior to first contact there are said to have been 112 million Native Americans in the Americas.[6] After contact and attempts at genocide against Native Americans that number has been dramatically reduced to 5.2 million of Native Americans combined with another race(s) and 2.9 million who identify only as American Indian or Alaskan Native.[7] A part of the history known by many in the United States but often forgotten is that this country was founded, in large measure, on the pursuit of religious freedom by those escaping religious persecution in their home countries. Meanwhile, a counternarrative, which is often lost in the historical narrative, is that those escaping religious persecution also persecuted the Indigenous peoples of this land in order to "eliminate" their "savage" ways and help them become civilized.

The usual narrative also fails to acknowledge the impact that Christianity and missionaries had on tribal communities. While each denomination took a portion of the United States to Christianize and did missionary work *on* the Indigenous peoples of that region, that work was allowed and encouraged

---

6   William M. Denevan, *The Native Population of the Americas in 1492,* 2nd ed. (Madison: University of Wisconsin Press, 1992).

7   Tina Norris, Paula L. Vines, and Elizabeth M. Hoeffel, "The American Indian and Alaska Native Population, 2010," *American Census Brief* (United States Census Bureau, 2012), http://www.census.gov/prod/cen2010/briefs/c2010br-10.pdf.

by the US government.[8] In addition, that mission work was done in a way that often told Indigenous peoples to cut their hair, not speak their language, and lose their cultural connections, because Christianity and Native American culture and language could not exist in one place. So, within a few generations many tribal languages, ceremonies, and ways of being were lost or modified for future generations of tribal peoples, communities, and families. Acknowledging the history and impact of Christianity on Native Americans and finding ways to accurately educate denominations, congregations, and clergy will start a movement to dispel myths and better help us move forward and learn how to work together, despite the historical traumas that persist. To acknowledge the past is to start the healing process and begin conversation about two cultures—Christian and Native American—with their various languages; both can exist in the same space and breathe freely if they want to.

The Oklahoma Indian Missionary Conference

The Oklahoma Indian Missionary Conference (OIMC) began as the forced removal of Indian tribes from the southeast and other parts of the United States to what was then Indian Territory. It was there that some of the newly formed congregations helped some of the tribes rebuild their own communities in the late nineteenth and early twentieth centuries.[9] Within this region Christians from some denominations and specifically those who identify as United Methodists were more sensitive to the languages and cultures and began building relationships with the thirty tribes. In 1972 the General Conference acknowledged OIMC as a missionary conference and gave it the same status as any other annual conference within the UMC.[10] The OIMC now consists of over eighty-four local churches in Kansas, Oklahoma, and

---

8   Clara Sue Kidwell, Homer Noley, and George E. Tinker, *A Native American Theology* (Maryknoll, NY: Orbis Books, 2001). Steven Charleston and Elaine A. Robinson, *Coming Full Circle: Constructing Native Christian Theology* (Minneapolis: Fortress Press, 2015).

9   T. Roughface, "Self-determination in Oklahoma," *Response* (Nov. 1970): 7–8.

10 "About Us," Oklahoma Indian Missionary Conference, accessed on Mar. 22, 2018, http://www.umc-oimc.org/resources/about-us.

Texas with more than six thousand members. Membership includes elders, adults, young adults, and children who represent most of the tribes in Oklahoma and many other tribal nations and home communities.

Reconciliation and Act of Repentance in The United Methodist Church

In 2000, individuals and committees within The UMC began to plan an Act of Repentance for the entire denomination. First, this acknowledgement process was meant to help local churches and congregations build relationships with local Native American communities, whether tribal or urban, in order to formally recognize the harm and impact on Native American communities. The next step was finding ways to remain connected and honor the history and contributions of the Indigenous peoples within the area. This Act of Repentance was envisioned as only a first step toward seeking forgiveness for the historic wrongs that have been done to Native Americans by United Methodists as well as encouraging even more steps toward reconciliation and relationship building with Native Americans within the annual conferences or anywhere our congregations and church members find themselves. It is important to note that the hope is that these Acts of Repentance and other consequent steps taken will create a pathway to healing for tribal and broader Native American communities, their young adults, and future generations of leaders within tribal communities as well as the OIMC.

Section II: Current Opportunities for Native American Young Adults

Opportunities within the OIMC

There are many opportunities for Native American young adults within The UMC and the OIMC. The OIMC has some colleges and universities in Oklahoma that have Native-based campus ministries, some of which have been in existence for years and some of which have emerged more recently. In each setting, however, the goal is to foster and develop ministries that nurture and honor Native American culture for young adults and college students.

These campus ministries are unique because they accept Native beliefs and culture and include serving food on a regular basis for Native American college students and accepting Native spirituality and cultural expressions. These ministries are not just about studying the Bible but are places that show how we live our Native spirituality through ceremonies and communal interactions.

These activities can include serving home-cooked or Native-style foods (traditional foods served for specific tribes or general foods like fry bread or Indian tacos), providing time for social activities such as bingo, Native (or tribal) hymn singing, and cultural activities, such as having sweats (a Native American ceremony that includes being in an enclosure while you sweat with hot rocks and prayer), Native American church services at the end of the semester, and blessing ceremonies for students as they begin or end their academic year. Another unique yet important component of these Native-based campus ministries is provided by a father, mother, uncle, or auntie figure, even if students see them only once a week, twice a month, or once a month. Being able to provide family-like support structures for Native American college students and young adults who are far from their own families speaks to an important cultural value and is foundational within the community. These important people help create that familial connection that many Native students are missing after moving away from their home and tribal or home communities.

Emerging from these campus ministries and in addition to them are the gatherings of Native American young adults at various UMC camps and other locations in the State of Oklahoma that provide a place to connect, get to know one another, and find ways to advocate for social issues that impact the surrounding tribal communities. The OIMC has also hosted and sponsored spring break trips that have allowed Native American young adults to be of service to the local community or other communities affected by natural disasters, such as the trip they took in 2005 in response to Hurricanes Katrina and Rita, which nearly devastated the United Houma Nation and community. This particular trip was remarkable, because it was an opportunity to serve and support other communities in a way that was balanced and not indicative of a "savior" complex. Ministry was done in a way that was reciprocal, honoring the culture and values of the Houma who lost so many physical possessions while sharing their culture and food.

Other opportunities have provided young adult Native American fellow-ships in urban areas, where they can find a church home and community. These fellowships have allowed a more flexible and less structured way of convening while also providing examples of what church can look like in terms of Native American worship and language. Local pastors, clergy, and laypersons have supported these fellowships. However, because of the lack of structure, these groups are prone to instability and need continual support by The UMC and OIMC. Despite these limitations, this type of fellowship can be a pathway and mechanism to engage Native American young adults and help their families to find a church home and a connection to traditional structures of church.

Opportunities within The UMC

It is important to note that there are broader opportunities within The UMC for Native American young adults, and their participation is determined by whether they are informed about them and if they feel they have a place at the table to share their spirituality while honoring who they are as Native Americans. There are opportunities within The UMC that run across the various general agencies of the church, but most are within the General Board of Higher Education and Ministry (GBHEM), although the General Board of Global Ministries (GBGM) has a summer internship program that matches Native American young adults with a specific Native community (urban or reservation), and the US-2 program under the Global Fellows program that allows young adults ages twenty to thirty to serve for two years within local Indigenous communities including states such as Oklahoma, Washington, Missouri, and Wisconsin.

In addition, GBHEM offers many scholarships that Native American students can apply for, for example the HANA scholarship and a Native American seminary scholarship, which provide funding resources for students on their higher education journey. Other opportunities include events such as

Exploration and What's Next? and funding from the Young Clergy Initiative.[11] It is important to note that it is more difficult to get Native American young adults to attend these events if they have to go alone; rather it is more comfortable for them to attend in groups or pairs. But at these events, it has been rare to have Native Americans acknowledged or a part of the planning team.

Only recently have there been more intentional efforts to acknowledge the Indigenous and tribal peoples within local venues and locations. So, while there are opportunities to engage with The UMC and its general agencies, communication about these events has been insufficient, and this might account for the lack of participation by Native Americans.

A Personal Narrative

As an Indigenous person, it is important for me to contextualize my own connections. I have been connected to The UMC since I was born. My grandfather served as a local pastor within the OIMC for over thirty-nine years and my grandmother was a member of the United Methodist Women (UMW). That meant that I grew up OIMC in its churches and Annual Conference. As a child who grew up close to my grandparents, I was able to attend various services with them, including funerals and weddings, and go to training events such as those on mission sponsored by the UMW, which were held across Oklahoma. Needless to say, this is the only church and Annual Conference I have ever known. Both of my grandparents were fluent speakers of the Kiowa language and they embedded that in their Native hymns as they sought to uphold strong community values, such as providing food to others, attending to the sick, remaining faithful through hard times, and giving selflessly to those they served.

Meanwhile, I have also seen the impact that the church has had on my grandparents. The indoctrination of the early local pastors in the OIMC and UMC who were Native American included being told that they had to choose which culture they would acknowledge and follow, and that their

---

11   Information on these opportunities can be found at: http://www.gbhem.org/education/student-portal.

known culture was not of the church or from the church. This was especially true when my grandfather first became a pastor in the mid-1950s. This type of thinking affected not only my grandparents but their children and grandchildren. While pastors like my grandfather were proud of their role in the church, their service to the community, and the church's help for Native Americans, their theology often minimized their own culture in those early days of the OIMC and The UMC in Oklahoma. I was not able to conceptualize or see this until I became a young adult, when I did a summer internship on the White Earth reservation in Minnesota.

During my internship, I was placed at a local church that incorporated the use of a ceremonial pipe including the use of tobacco at the beginning of their service to honor who they were as Anishinaabe, meaning "the original people." Early Europeans called them Ojibwe, but when others could not pronounce this, they were then called Chippewa.[12] My internship was an awakening moment for me as I saw it was OK to incorporate my culture into my spiritual practices and beliefs as a Christian and United Methodist. From there, my understanding of connecting our tribal culture and Christianity became broader and more open. I learned that we have a space, even if we have to create that space or be a part of those gatherings with all of their discomfort and "itchiness." So as a Native American young adult, I was able to participate in the Native-based campus ministries through my university and find a home place at an OIMC local church. I was also able to participate in UMC-related events such as the GBGM summer internship with the White Earth reservation, attend the UM Student Forum three times, attend Exploration, and receive a HANA scholarship. Later as a Native American student-affairs professional, I was able to support a Native-based campus ministry at my own institution and then cocreate a Native American young adult fellowship that is still operating in Albuquerque. I have also been able to serve two quadrennia on the GBHEM Board of Directors and share my voice and perspective as a Native American woman and young adult.

---

12 https://whiteearth.com/history.

This narrative demonstrates the connections that I have with The UMC and OIMC, and this chapter is a testimony that people can give back and find space, even when you sometimes have to create your own space and find your voice so that Native Americans will be acknowledged and a part of the conversation. We have been displaced on our own homelands for too long; it is now time we hear what will be the future of The UMC and OIMC and how to create spaces while honoring the culture and lived realities of Native Americans.

Section III: A Counter-Narrative and Insight as Told through the Voices of Native American Young Adults

Method

To give voice to Native American young adult experience, I conducted a study, which utilized a mixed-methods approach including both qualitative and quantitative approaches. The recruitment method was via purposive and snowball sampling. Purposive and snowball sampling means that I worked with the OIMC superintendent to identify participants in order to send an outreach email recruitment letter. A criterion for participants was that they were Native American young adults who had participated in programs or events sponsored by the OIMC or The UMC in the last five years. Once participants agreed, they received the link to an online survey and were given two weeks to respond.

The survey used a Likert scale and open-ended questions. The validated instrument uses and references other Likert scales that seek to understand the lived experience of college students. Open-ended questions and words that can be used to describe the participant's experience are in the respondent's Indigenous language along with the English equivalent. The analysis process was done once all of the surveys had been completed. This included compiling charts and averaging the Likert scale responses and using the open-ended responses to code themes, to better understand the lived experiences of the Native American young adults and to gather their recommendations and feedback.

Participants

Participants were Native American (federally or state recognized) young adults affiliated with the OIMC. The participant enrollment included sixteen Native American young adults who completed an online survey. The tribal nations that the Native American young adults represented were: Kiowa (3), Muskogee Creek (2), Maskoke (1), Chickasaw (1), Mississippi Choctaw (1), Ponca (1), Choctaw (2), Comanche (2), Seminole (2), and Sac and Fox (1). There were also responses in which the Native American young adults indicated multiple tribal affiliations. It is more common in Oklahoma for Native Americans to identify with more than one tribe or they are likely to list more than one. I left this open so that it was up to the discernment of the person answering how many tribes he or she identified and listed.

Findings, Results, and Recommendations

1. What Is Your Place in The United Methodist Church and the OIMC?

It was important to know how long the participants had been connected to The United Methodist Church. The average length of time connected was 23 years. The majority of respondents have been connected to The UMC for most or all of their lives. There were two who were only connected to The UMC for the last four years, most likely during their undergraduate degree and time at the university. One respondent said he/she had been connected to The UMC since "1830 or possibly before," indicating their ancestors' connection.

A follow-up question asked about the length of time that each person was or had been connected to the OIMC. The average length of time connected to the OIMC was 23 years. It is important to note that only a few had been involved with the OIMC all of their lives and a few had been involved for 4 or 5 years.

There were two questions about the length of time that each person was or had been connected with the OIMC and The UMC. Although the OIMC and The UMC are related, often it is easier for Native Americans to understand the connection they clearly have to the OIMC and less so with

The UMC as a denomination, because the Native perspective is often left out or invisible in the outreach and connections in the broader programming and ministries.

2. Deep and Loose Connections

It is important to see not only how long the Native American young adults have been a part of the OIMC and The UMC but also how old they are, that is how long they have been involved in the church as a young adult. It also of interest to see how this averages as compared with The UMC's definition of a young adult, which is someone ages 18–35. The average number of years of participation is 7.8 years. The highest number of years involved was 18 for two of the participants; 16 and 13 for one. Next, the young adults were asked to rate their level of involvement ranging from 1 (least involved) to 5 (very involved). Results revealed: 1, least involved: 12.5%; 2, somewhat involved: 6.5%; 3, neutral: 25%; 4, involved: 43.75%; and 5, very involved: 12.5%. The highest ratings were for neutral, involved, and very involved. These responses and answers reflect whether the Native American young adults see themselves as having deep and close connections within the OIMC and The UMC.

3. Finding Space

In this section, Native American young adults rated their experiences with OIMC and UMC young adult–related events; how they have seen their Native American culture incorporated into The UMC- and/or OIMC-related young adult events; and whether they have found space in the OIMC- and UMC-related young adult events or programs. Lastly, the Native American young adults shared their experiences as related to some of the events in which they had participated. It is important to remember the relevance of space within Native American culture. Space in tribal communities is intricately tied to the spaces of their origin and inhabitation. Native American communities followed the seasons and honored the Earth in ways that were deeply connected in spirituality and being. The impact of having space, whether physical or figurative as acknowledging and honoring their presence, is not new but rather ancestral and speaks to who we are as Indigenous peoples.[13]

The current or recent Native American young adults rated their experiences within The UMC- or OIMC-related young adult events. The results were: 1, very dissatisfied: 0%; 2, dissatisfied: 6.25%; 3, neutral: 12.50%; 4, somewhat satisfied: 31.25%; and 5, very satisfied: 50%. This outcome was not predictable when placing both The UMC- and OIMC-related young adult events together, since many times they are looked at separately. A couple Native American young adults said that they weren't very involved but would have liked to be more involved. Another commented that it would be nice to see more events but he/she understood the challenges, and one said that there were "very few young adults involved" and "not very many OIMC young adult events." Then others said that they have participated in Bible studies, mission trips, and the annual OIMC young adult event gatherings. Another said that his/her participation in the United Methodist Student Movement was life changing, because he/she saw how Christians are called to engage in social justice. Last, one shares a more thorough response to the impact of UMC- and OIMC-related young adult events: "I am satisfied with UMC and OIMC young adult events. Though the two experiences are completely separate. My experience with UMC young adult events revolves around fellowship and entertainment. OIMC related young adult events also have fellowship, but often come with a charge to affect change within their tribes and communities. There is an underlying responsibility inherent in OIMC young adult events because of the struggle to keep our cultures alive and vibrant." Responses that make connections to Native American culture and tribal identity are powerful and telling.

In understanding the context of ratings, it is important to understand how or if the Native American young adults saw their Native American/

---

13 Vine Deloria Jr. and James Treat, *For This Land: Writings on Religion in America* (New York: Routledge, 1999); Vine Deloria Jr. and Daniel R. Wildcat, *Power and Place: Indian Education in America* (Golden, CO: Fulcrum Pub., 2001); Kidwell, Noley, and Tinker, *A Native American Theology.*

tribal culture incorporated into UMC- or OIMC-related young adult events. The following demonstrates the level of perceived representation of Native American/tribal culture: 1, not incorporated: 0%; 2, somewhat incorporated: 31.25%; 3, neutral: 6.25%: 4, incorporated: 43.75%; and 5, very incorporated: 18.75%. Within this question, there was opportunity for the participants to provide more insight into the types of events and activities in which they have participated as Native American young adults. The ways that the Native American young adults saw their Native American culture incorporated at the OIMC level included having tribal language classes, Native American Church ceremonies, tribal hymns, instruction in making a traditional (tribal) dress, learning how to cook traditional (tribal) foods, and stories. At a broader level within the OIMC not directly connected to Native American culture, events that were mentioned were physical activities such as basketball, games, college visits, and leading a service by young adults. The responses about how these Native American young adults see their culture represented in The UMC included not seeing any Native American culture or only seeing a tribal hymn incorporated in a UMC hymnbook. These examples of the types of incorporation of Native American culture point to why Native American young adults do not see themselves connected to The UMC in general.

After looking at how Native American young adults rate their experiences with OIMC and UMC young adult–related events and how or if they see their Native American culture incorporated, the next logical question is if they found space in the OIMC- or UMC-related young adult events. The responses to this question were that 87.50% felt they found space and 12.50% said they did not find space. It is important to note that the question combined The UMC and OIMC. So the results might be different if the questions separated The UMC and OIMC.

The survey also gave participants opportunity to provide additional comments. The comments depended on the young adult level of participation; if or when there were young adult events, and whether they saw space. One comment provides insight and understanding: "Yes, but I consider my involvement in the OIMC young adult events to be separate from the broader UMC young adult events. At times it feels that, aside from doctrine, the OIMC is only tangentially related to the general UMC. I realize that this may be due to the size of the conference in comparison to the rest of the Church body."

Last, it is important to understand in which type of events the Native American young adults have participated within the OIMC and The UMC. Some of the events listed at the OIMC level areas: campus ministry by Native American laity and pastors, tribal hymn singings, baby moccasin–making classes, young adult retreats, sweats, Native American Church meetings, OIMC day, powwows, OIMC-led mission trips to tribal communities, OIMC young adult banquets, and OIMC Annual Conference. UMC events that were attended included serving on United Methodist Student Movement boards, General Board of Global Ministry internship, Exploration and/or US-2, General Conference, and the Acts of Repentance ceremony at General Conference.

Recommendations for The UMC and OIMC

The survey asked for recommendations to incorporate to acknowledge Native American young adults in UMC programs/events and in OIMC programs/events. The question separated the OIMC and UMC so that the voice of Native American young adults could be heard in both contexts.

The specific recommendations for The UMC included suggestions about how to incorporate Native American young adult input and create more space for them in the broader denomination. Suggestions ranged from: "every event/program needs to have a young adult and youth representative"; "create a student leadership group that informs the programming for young adults"; "have a Native American young adult serve in the group"; "make sure the programming does not conflict, so men and women don't have to choose between being in those groups"; "do more than just welcome and acknowledge the Indigenous peoples of that area as a ceremony by incorporating some of the groups and people in the event"; "have local young adult groups from dominant UMC churches interact with Native American young adult groups to provide education about Native Americans and participate in a cultural event"; and in connection to this "host workshops on history of Native Americans and how Christianity became a part of their culture." Some additional suggestions include: "Do not be afraid of hearing the theological voices of young adults. . . . We have a yearning for cultural reclamation and many of us do not want to have to forego our generational relationship to the UMC, resulting from theological intolerance, especially considering that the church has become a part of our heritage as well (namely via OIMC)."

There are Native American young adults who have been educated in theology and can contribute to transforming what currently exists to add and deepen the Indigenous perspective in what currently exists. Some pivotal questions posed by one of the Native American young adults as a recommendation for consideration include:

> To me the two sides of this question are as follows: Do we work to bring The UMC to Indian Country and generate an effect by exposure to the realities of OIMC Young Adults. Alternatively, do we work on bringing OIMC young adults into the general UMC events to be leaders and thereby generate a change by way of their cultural insight. Truthfully, I believe that the former option would be difficult to achieve, because of the remoteness of many OIMC churches. I recommend finding young adults in the OIMC and supporting them financially and spiritually as they participate in UMC events.

This is one immediate possibility for getting more Native American young adults in the broader UMC events and programming for young adults. Another important observation for The UMC to consider in the outreach and increase of participation comes from another respondent:

> There seems to be a big push for more young adult involvement, but not as much for minority young adults. The church has been stressing the importance of having young adults in the church who will be the leaders one day, however it doesn't seem that they care much for the future of ethnic leaders in the church.

For this one Native American young adult to observe this despite recent efforts to increase young adult participation in the UMC suggests that it is likely other Native American young adults see this as well. Given these responses, how can The UMC and its agencies increase the participation of Native American young adults now that they have received these recommendations?

So, what are the recommendations for the OIMC about how to incorporate or acknowledge tribal-specific culture in their general programs/events? The recommendations that were specific regarding culture were to have Tribal elders help with language, storytelling, arts and crafts; have a printed paraphrased translation of tribal songs; incorporate more tribal traditions in the events; and consider having monthly dinners or gatherings for Native American young adults.

Affirmation of some of these suggestions for OIMC events for Native American young adults include:

> OIMC has a tradition of several things which I find helpful for the students: campus ministry dinners, socials, sweats, elder visits, NAC meetings, tribal singings. The OIMC cannot in itself recreate an entire culture, but by providing authentic spiritual, emotional, and other kinds of support will nourish many students, regardless of tribal affiliation.

Another Native American young adult addressed how some elders have been taught that tribal tradition does not belong in church. "Elders who believe tribal traditions do not belong in the church need education that these tribal traditions do have a place." A way to address beliefs about whether tribal traditions can have a place in the OIMC could happen through the intergenerational interaction between youth, young adults, and elders. Or as was said by one respondent:

> To have more youth interaction throughout conferences. When youth are involved it brings a different vibe to the atmosphere on both parts of adults and youth. Since youth are the next leaders it's a good experience to have them interact with the adults to learn what goes on, but to show the adults the way they are learning the culture through singing hymns, sign language, story-telling, or other activities.

A way to address these suggestions is to scrutinize and decolonize the prior teachings of Christianity that say that Native American culture is inferior or does not belong in the church:

Begin to engage more progressive theologies and begin deviating at a faster pace from early missionary rhetoric that postures our traditional culture as inferior to Christianity, which is inherently linked to Western civilization and the notion of superiority/supremacy. I want to see OIMC encounter our traditional cosmologies and other philosophical worldviews without needing to justify such practices and beliefs through a Eurocentric Christian lens. In order to get there, OIMC would need to abandon its evangelicalism/fundamentalism. I recommend OIMC start by engaging decolonization practices and introspective analysis.

Critical Closure and Beginning the Healing Process

The beginning of this chapter provided an overview of the background of Native Americans in higher education and contextualized the current state in which Native American young adults find themselves in regard to access and services. It also provided a brief comment on the historical background of Christianity, missionaries and The United Methodist Church, the OIMC, and the reconciliation and Acts of Repentance. Some might still wonder why all this is important. The reality is that many who are not surrounded by Native American tribes or do not have connections to them are not aware of how this history impacts the current state of Native peoples and their perceptions of The UMC. Showing how Native American young adults connect to the broader UMC and the OIMC and why it's important to acknowledge our own or my own journey within the OIMC is another layer of understanding. Finally, so readers could hear Native American young adult voices, I shared a study that recorded the thoughts of Native American young adults and allowed them to share their own experiences within the OIMC and UMC, how they see their culture acknowledged and if they find space in the church.

The study suggests that while they may believe in their own tribal stories, they also acknowledge that Jesus died for their sins. They want to speak their own voice and experience pride in who they are as Native Americans. They want to honor their culture as much as they love God. Native American young adults want to know, now that The UMC has agreed to honor the complex relationship and hurtful history of The UMC and Native peoples through the Act of Repentance, how will we take the next step and how will The UMC acknowledge the living ancestors of those survivors of this hurtful history to support and develop a new generation of Indigenous leaders for the church and their respective communities?

OUT OF JOINT
The Dislocation of Our Bodies from the Church's Sexual Ethic

Timothy S. Moore

Director of Donor Relations, Office of Advancement,
Union Presbyterian Seminary

> We affirm that sexuality is God's good gift to all persons. . . .
> We affirm that all persons are individuals of sacred worth,
> created in the image of God. . . . The United Methodist
> Church does not condone the practice of homosexuality and
> considers this practice incompatible with Christian teaching.

Something does not feel quite right. Something about the epigraph to this chapter, taken from *The Book of Discipline of the United Methodist Church*, feels disjointed. In that statement, homosexuals, according to *The Discipline*,[1] are both individuals of sacred worth yet barred from practices corresponding with homosexuality. In a single paragraph,[2] a jarring juxtaposition

---

1   *The Book of Discipline of the United Methodist Church, 2016* (Nashville: The United Methodist Publishing House, 2016), ¶161, 112–13. Hereafter abbreviated as *The Discipline*.

2   "Paragraph" is a technical term deployed by the church to reference different sections of *The Discipline*. Throughout this text, this technical term will be used following that disciplinary pattern.

occurs. The United Methodist Church[3] affirms homosexuals along with all persons then almost immediately abuts that affirmation with a statement of substantial delimitation. How can this be? How can the church speak of homosexuals as being individuals of sacred worth followed by an unqualified condemnation of all the practices of homosexuality? Is the church assuming that what *constitutes* homosexuality (and its being categorized as a subset within the gift of all sexuality) is devoid of any practices *commensurate* with homosexuality? In other words, do our practices matter to who we are? Is one heterosexual or homosexual because of inclinations or actions or both?[4] Which represents the church's position, and does it, ultimately, matter?

It is my contention that it does matter, because actions demonstrate who we fundamentally are. In the end, what underlies the church's statements on human sexuality and how the church is able comfortably to separate statements of who we are from statements about what we do is because of thought constructs originating with philosophical modernity. These thought constructs allow detachment, immutability, and immateriality to take the lead in our theological reasoning at the cost of covenantal connectedness, habituated malleability, and indispensable embodiment.

This reliance upon modernity is problematic for several reasons. First, modernity's thought constructs seem to be in opposition to other fundamental theological practices and claims important to our church's theological heritage, namely our notions of Incarnation, the Eucharist, and sanctification. That opposition creates an internal disjunction, causing the parts of our theology on sexuality to misalign with those fundamental theological practices and claims. Second, at least with regard to its statements on human sexuality, the church is still living in modernity while the world has moved on

---

3   Hereafter, The United Methodist Church will generally be abbreviated as The UMC or simply "the church."

4   It is important to note that while using the categories of "heterosexual" and "homosexual" above I am not assuming a simple sexual binary exists. Rather, sexuality, sexual attraction, gender, and other attending issues seem far more complex than such a facile construal. As my larger argument seeks to disrupt the conceptualization of these categories apart from our habituated bodies, such a binary conceptualization will be rendered irrelevant given the linkage of who we are with what we do. Here, these categories act as simple placeholders to mark our entry into the conversation.

into postmodernity. And if the church is to remain relevant, especially when it comes to social issues, it needs to expand its horizons, reorienting its language and reasoning. To be fair, this Disciplinary statement is less the result of reflective theology than impromptu group editing.[5] Nevertheless, its sloppy conceptual articulation provides a way into an important conversation for the church to help it explore the issue of human sexuality more intentionally.

Not wanting to dismiss the issues related to homosexuality, my intent is to better attend to them by sweeping them into a broader conversation about human sexuality. In particular, my more specific interest is exploring the theological issue of sexuality by considering the indispensability of bodies and embodied practices in how we understand what it means to be human. Embodied performances and stories should have priority in shaping our reflective systems of thought.[6] However, the presence of essentialist language within the church's claims about sexuality might suggest a reverse strategy at work in our church's sexual ethic. The church seems to be laboring to articulate appropriate (holy) sexual habits and our (theological) anthropology apart from or before contemplating our bodies and embodied practices.

There appear to be essentialist claims underlying the church's assumptions about sexuality. The lure of certainty accompanying essentialist claims remains attractive because of a confidence in their presumed immutability, a presumption I will address shortly. Yet, in the end, it seems that essentialist claims are inherently "unchristian," because of their latent gnostic consequences. Bodies require a fundamental and primal place in our theology and in our understandings of human sexuality because of the scriptural witness to the Incarnation

5   Gary L. Ball-Kilbourne, *The Church Studies Homosexuality* (Nashville: Cokesbury, 1994), 11. Here, the study commission's report notes that this paragraph, specifically what was to become known as the "incompatibility clause," was added in floor debate at the 1972 General Conference plenary session.

6   For a more robust account of the relationship between performance, stories, and reflective systems, see my thoughts in "Sunesis: Understanding via Interplay," in Matthew W. Charlton and Kathy M. Armistead, eds., *The Prophetic Voice and Making Peace* (Nashville: GBHEM Publishing, 2016). Such systems of thought are important but always emerge from our prior performances and stories. For instance, historical criticism, as a discipline, only gains its efficacy after events have been lived and a narrative construed to render those events into a coherent whole. We call that system of reflection issuing from those events and that narrative "historical criticism." And that system of reflection is not possible, cannot come into being without them.

and the centrality granted to the practice of the Eucharist. Both the witness to the Incarnation and the practice of the Eucharist undergird and substantiate the church's general notions about what it means to be human—that is, its theological anthropology—and what humans should do—that is, our ethics. The Incarnation and the Eucharist tell us that our bodies are important and the practices, which include sexual practices, of those bodies must be important and indispensable to any articulation of a holy life and holy thoughts about that life. Importantly, I am not saying that habits should not be regulated or some promoted while others discouraged. Rather, what I am saying is that when speaking about human sexuality and sexuality habits those claims should follow from our more primary claims about the Incarnation, the Eucharist, and sanctification. I will argue that to offer the good news of Jesus Christ requires that the church intentionally consider how we speak *about* and *with* persons of all sexualities inside and outside the church, particularly as we seek to speak faithfully and clearly on college and university campuses.

Making this argument involves several steps. *First*, the official body of thought around human sexuality offered by the church must be assembled and examined. I will trace the broad contours created by some of The UMC's statements on human sexuality, generally, and homosexuality, particularly. This body of thought is scattered but has distinct features. I will bring some order by marking a common feature that recurs in the language of the church's statements. That feature points to a certain theological anthropology embedded in the church's notion of human sexuality, which betrays a latent commitment to essentialism and philosophical foundationalism. This commitment is problematic because, as I mentioned above, it relies upon thought constructs allowing detachment, immutability, and immateriality to take the lead in our theological reasoning at the cost of covenantal connectedness, habituated malleability, and indispensable embodiment. This loss of connectedness, malleability, and embodiment disjoin our theology of human sexuality from other inviolable theological commitments of the church.

Second, I will refine my argument through a diagnostic critique of foundationalism, its supportive story—that is, the standard account—and that story's disembodied protagonist or anthropology—that is, the *humanum*. I will offer a more complete picture of both that account and its anthropology below. The impact of the standard account and the humanum on the church's understanding of human sexuality and sexual ethic is subtle yet pervasive. Through this line of reasoning, I will clarify what I mean when I say "homosexual" or "heterosexual," coming to understand those claims as statements descriptive of social habits and physical practices rather than fixed descriptions assigned to a person's fundamental self.[7]

Third, I will hint at a prescription to remedy this problem, suggesting the alternative outcome that our denominational conversations can have if we begin with an idea of embodied practices, the community that can be assumed, and a narrative grounded in flesh and blood rather than abstract reflection. These embodied practices and the alternative story can replace the story of the standard account with the story of the gospel and the performance of the humanum with that of the *eschaton adam*. In the end, what I offer is an examination of those issues that affect the body ecclesia and its doctrinal claims.

Examination: A Disjointed Body

Our examination begins with a short rehearsal of the church's scattered and disjointed body of statements on human sexuality, generally, and homosexuality, particularly. I will work to bring some order marking that common feature that recurs in the language of the church's statements. That feature points to a particular theological anthropology embedded in the church's

---

7   Homosexuality and heterosexuality are not simply categories pertaining to an individual's physical attraction to persons of the same or the opposite gender. In fact, there is much debate as to what these descriptions do explain and how effective they are. Are they descriptions of involuntary physiological responses to visual and physical stimuli? Are they more appropriately understood as descriptions of individuals' behavior? Can this behavior be limited to a particular time in a person's life, or do they describe a person's entire life? Are these descriptions an effort to name personal preference, irrespective of behaviors while exclusively referencing an orientation? Interestingly, Simon LeVay asks a similar series of questions in his own work, attempting to ascertain precisely what it is that various researchers into homosexuality presume when they engage in their work. Such presumed meaning(s) of homosexuality will invariably, LeVay argues, shape both the structure and results of our research. Being aware of this influence of presumed meaning(s) is critical for our work to be properly communicated and disparate results accurately compared. Simon LeVay, *Queer Science: The Use and Abuse of Research into Homosexuality* (Cambridge: MIT Press, 1996), 45–46.

conceptualization of human sexuality. In the long run, I intend to substitute a more theologically appropriate anthropology for the one the church currently uses for its assumptions about human sexuality. As mentioned, this current anthropology betrays a latent commitment to essentialism and philosophical foundationalism, both concepts I will draw into focus, here, and will subsequently explain more fully in the following section.

Statements

The most significant and contested statement on homosexuality by the church is found in the Social Principles. Not church law but certainly authoritative, the Social Principles are meant significantly to influence those portions of church law that are binding. And as numerous Judicial Council rulings attest, they do. This being said, a subsection of the Social Principles addresses a variety of topics intended to further the work of the church by "nurturing human beings into the fullness of their humanity."[8] In that section—a section already referenced above—the church speaks about human sexuality generally and homosexuality specifically:

> We affirm that sexuality is God's good gift to all persons. We call everyone to responsible stewardship of this sacred gift. . . . We affirm that all persons are individuals of sacred worth, created in the image of God. All persons need the ministry of the Church in their struggles for human fulfillment. . . . The United Methodist Church does not condone the practice of homosexuality and considers this practice incompatible with Christian teaching.[9]

This statement requires some unpacking. For instance, if someone is homosexual, how is his or her "sacred worth" related to his or her actions being incompatible with Christian teaching? The church does not recognize, at least such seems to be the case from this statement, how sexual practices might contribute to self-identity, to *fulfillment* of our humanity, given that every specific sexual practice related to homosexuality is rendered incompatible

---

8   *The Discipline, 2016,* ¶161, 110.

9   *The Discipline, 2016,* ¶161, 112–13.

and rejected. In such a conceptualization of sexuality, as the church presently renders it, specific sexual practices peculiar to who one is (or might be) seem inconsequential. Importantly, I am not saying that we are only the sum total of our actions. What it means to be human certainly includes more than just doing. Yet, at the same time, I am saying that we cannot be understood in any fundamental way devoid of our actions.

Moreover, it is important to note the significance that the church assumes human sexuality has in someone's ability to be *fully* human. Such a claim by the church suggests an ontological primacy for heterosexuality and homosexuality. By ontological primacy, I am referring to that part or those parts that make people who they are in a fundamental, identifiable, insoluble way. And, following such a logical construal as couched in the church's current statements, the descriptors "heterosexuality" and "homosexuality" seem to be first, fixed, and foundational. These descriptions do not emerge from practices but seem to be able to stand alone from any particular or related practices. The above Disciplinary statement certainly appears to imply that our sexuality has a significant role in constituting the self. If these observations prove accurate, then why the church is willing to make such an anthropological claim when speaking about sexuality yet is unwilling to do so when speaking about Christian perfection and sanctification, two concepts to which I will turn shortly, must be asked.

The church's conceptual understanding of human sexuality is further nuanced by a second statement in the Social Principles concerning the church's support of equal rights.

> Equal Rights Regardless of Sexual Orientation—Certain basic human rights and civil liberties are due all persons. We are committed to supporting those rights and liberties for homosexual persons. We see a clear issue of simple justice in protecting their rightful claims where they have shared material resources, pensions, guardian relationships, mutual powers of attorney, and other such lawful claims typically attendant to contractual relationships that involve shared contributions, responsibilities, and liabilities, and equal protection before the law.[10]

---

10 *The Discipline, 2016*, ¶162, 123.

This statement on human rights underscores the church's assumption that human sexuality, generally, is easily and necessarily divorced from any sexual habits given that the church finds it comfortably congruous simultaneously to reject practices exclusively associated or even definitive of homosexuality while supporting broadly all sorts of rights for homosexual persons. Such a position only seems tenable if persons and their actions may be substantively disjoined.

More important, in contrast to the claims about human sexuality, in statements on Christian perfection and sanctification, actions seem to be consequential to who we are. Actions seem to shape us fundamentally. More specifically, in a paragraph from *The Discipline* directly addressing the theological concepts of sanctification and perfection, the church promotes an intentional link between perfection as "[fulfilling] human beings, who are called to covenant partnership with God"[11] and holy, embodied habits: "Sanctifying grace draws us toward the gift of Christian perfection, which Wesley described as a heart 'habitually filled with the love of God and neighbor' and as 'having the mind of Christ and walking as he walked.'"[12] Patently, this core theological concept for the church relies upon a nascent philosophical and anthropological assumption that a body habited in love is linked to human fulfillment.

Furthermore, in inquiring about the nature of the anthropology described in its statements about human sexuality, we might ask about the anthropological origins behind these claims. Are they Christologically grounded? If not, what is their grounding? These questions point to the heart of the matter: Does the church rely upon one set of anthropological commitments when speaking about sexuality and another when speaking about other matters of faith, for example, sanctification and perfection? In short, I think it does. Said more strongly, the anthropology undergirding the church's assertions about human sexuality is suspicious of claims that actions impact us in a fundamental way. In addition, that anthropology originates with

---

11 *The Discipline, 2016*, ¶102, 53.

12 *The Discipline, 2016*, ¶102, 55.

philosophical schools of thought—for example, Kantianism and other Enlightenment philosophies—that reject the notion that actions might affect who we are substantively. Kantianism and other Enlightenment philosophies evolved from claims about what it means to be human that are suspicious not only of particular actions but of embodiment, in general. The removal of who we are from what we do and what it means to have a body makes what we do with our bodies less consequential and more a matter of detached intellectual transaction. I will return to this concern later.

I have begun to identify some of the more problematic issues and inconsistencies within some formative statements by the church. That consistent use of a particular anthropology is problematic. That theological anthropology needs identifying and the strength, weaknesses, and validity of using that theological anthropology as a basis for doctrinal statements on human sexuality needs consideration. Having examined issues related to a latent theological anthropology, I turn to explore the consequences that this anthropology yields.

Foundationalism, the Standard Account, and the Humanum

> A system of knowledge is like a building, whose soundness depends on its foundation. If the foundation is not solid, it may need to be torn down and rebuilt on a new and stronger foundation. . . . But what is that foundation to be? The short answer is that there are only two options: Scripture and experience.[13]

In her assessment of the construction and faults in modernity's philosophical and theological edifice, Nancey Murphy reduces five centuries of Western Christian intellectual development into two camps of competing interpretative strategies, that is, the conservative camp with a preference for originating its claims via scripture and the liberal camp with a preference for originating its

---

13 Nancey Murphy, *Beyond Liberalism and Fundamentalism* (Newburgh, IN: Trinity Press International, 1996), 12.

claims via experience.[14] While certainly overly simplistic, Murphy's account proves useful for outlining the general edges and foci of these two herme-neutical representatives. Yet, what is most important in Murphy's account is not her generalization of what differentiates these strategies but her identifi-cation of what they hold in common. This commonality is modernity's reliance upon foundationalism. Foundationalism is the basis for many assumptions about what it means to be human, including those assumptions operative in The UMC's statements on human sexuality. As will be seen, being a physical body becomes secondary or inconsequential or possibly even problematic within such an intellectual system. This foundationalism is unfortunate and theologically flawed. I turn next to foundationalism and its consequences.

Foundationalism

Foundationalism describes a philosophical (and theological) preference for general, indisputable, and abstract truth claims that are not reliant upon par-ticular, local claims or commitments. Summarizing this point, Murphy deter-mines that, "[in] short, it is the quest of *universal* knowledge that drives the modern quest for *indubitable* foundations."[15] Birthed during a time of great social and intellectual disturbance, foundationalism endeavors to secure a degree of precision as to those philosophical (and theological) commitments that can stabilize truth claims in order to bring universal assent, social solidity, and a clear vision for right action. Thus, for Murphy, foundationalism has two defining features: (1) it includes beliefs that are immune from challenge and (2) holds that reason proceeds in one direction, from the universal certainty to particular expression and never the inverse.[16]

---

14 NB: The link between, on the one hand, modernity's philosophical preferences for either scripture or experience as the basis for making doctrinal claims and ethical decisions and, on the other hand, the contentious and divergent arguments proffered by "conservative" and "liberal" positions on human sexuality need hardly be mentioned. Both arguments are highly modern in origin and character, fol-lowing well-trod and expected lines of thought and discourse.

15 Murphy, *Beyond Liberalism*, 13; emphasis in the original.

16 Murphy, 13. The disjunction between these two features of foundationalism and the church's no-tions of sanctification and the Christian narrative are patent. For instance, sanctification is a doctrine that assumes mutability of the participants in the practices of holy living—a clear departure from

In Murphy's depiction, the original laborer who laid foundationalism's footings was René Descartes. His search for pure reason, devoid of particularities and potentially violent disputes, began with an exercise in rational deconstruction, using a form of intellectual regression to strip away particularity. This stripping, he asserted, allowed him to arrive at a foundation that rested on what he hoped would be unassailable certainty as codified in his formulation that *cogito ergo sum*.[17] Descartes's results seemed to supply theologians a reasonable and rational methodology for crafting religious assertions with a high level of clarity.

Following her discussion of Descartes, Murphy moves a few hundred miles west and more than a hundred years forward to John Locke, who took up Descartes's methodological approach. Locke's work produced not a single avenue to knowledge but a threefold approach, each approach complementary to the others and equally valid in witnessing to the same, common, universal, and indubitable truth.[18] These three kinds of knowledge included knowledge acquired through empirical science, deductive reasoning, and revelation.[19] A defining superstructure for modern thought emerged from Locke's epistemology and methodology, a superstructure with three supportive towers, each representing discrete yet connected core loci for articulating truth claims and for making definitive assertions about right living.

As we see from Murphy's depiction of foundationalism, modernity's foundationalism, it seems, underlies the church's reasoning. This modern thinking is evident in the church's dislocated conversations about sexuality and sexual acts and, more to the point, the church's elemental assumptions about the relationship between sexuality, sexual acts, bodies, and personal identity. Detachment, immutability, and immateriality take the lead at the cost of covenantal connectedness, habituated malleability, and embodiment.

---

foundationalism. Similarly, the Christian narrative relies upon a premise that particular expressions render the claims of the faith intelligible and are, essentially, devoid of substantive meaning apart from their particular claims.

17 Murphy, 14.

18 Murphy, 14.

19 Murphy, 14.

But before venturing to propose an alternative way forward for the church, another examination is required. Compounding the effects of foundationalism is a related malady, having an equally consequential impact on the denomination's deliberations—the standard account. The most prominent advocate for this account is Immanuel Kant.

The Standard Account and the Humanum

> I ought never to act except in such a way that I can also will that my maxim should become a universal law.[20]

> We still consider Kant the single most significant statement of the program implied by the standard account.[21]

The standard account is, as Stanley Hauerwas and David Burrell put it, primarily a narrative. Like all narratives its purpose is to collect disparate experiences and bits of data and organize them within a structure to create a cohesive and intelligible whole, thus rendering life and our perception of it reasonable. What makes the standard account "standard" is, as Hauerwas and Burrell maintain, the Enlightenment mandate to free morality and reason from "localized," "subjective" determinations.[22] In other words, the standard account claims to be the common account of reality, that is, it is *the* standard, against which all other accounts are measured. This liberation from particular constraints, according to Hauerwas, results in the necessary loss of other narratives that are grounded in their particularity.

> Liberalism [i.e., the standard account] in its many forms and versions, presupposes that society can be organized without any narrative that is commonly held to be true. As a result, it tempts us to believe that freedom and rationality are independent of narrative—i.e., we are free to the extent we have no story.[23]

---

20 Immanuel Kant, *Groundwork of the Metaphysic of Morals*, trans. H. J. Paton (New York: Harper and Row, 1964), 70.

21 Hauerwas and Burrell, "From System to Story," 173n21.

22 Hauerwas and Burrell, 160.

23 Stanley Hauerwas, *A Community of Character: Toward a Constructive Christian Social Ethic* (Notre Dame, IN: University of Notre Dame Press, 1981), 12.

The standard account's strength is its tendency to command loyalty to its message above and beyond other narrative commitments as it presents itself as a description of reality devoid of the many harmful restrictions characterizing other narrative claims. Yet, its weakness is couched in its strength. This narrative's contention that it is above other narratives overlooks the fact that it too is a particular narrative.

Thus, the standard account is the myth of reality substituted to replace competing, culturally, physically grounded narratives.[24] In this way, the standard account is a story that denies the existence of its own story and others' stories.[25] We can see this in Kant's construal of religious discourse and doctrine.[26] The particularities of narratives that give indispensable substance to our lives are the very conditions that the standard account defines as deleterious to moral and rational adjudication.[27] For this reason, the standard account narrates existence as an account that endeavors to distance itself from all parochial constraints, moving persons and their rationality and morality away from the particular and toward the general.[28] Therefore, what characterizes the standard account is (1) the abandonment of particularity for the sake of universally recognizable truth claims and (2) the rejection of narrative description in favor of detached, neutral principles that define and regulate life.[29] It follows then that within this schema, what fundamentally

---

24 Hauerwas, *A Community of Character*, 78.

25 Hauerwas and Burrell, "From System to Story," 173–76.

26 Immanuel Kant, *Religion within the Limits of Reason Alone*, trans. Theodore M. Greene and Hoyt H. Hudson (La Salle, IL: Open Court, 1960), 36. Time and space do not permit my giving the necessary attention to the importance of particularity for Hauerwas and his reading of Kant and Kant's resistance to the notion that particularity may have a determinative impact upon one's ethics. More work and space should and shall be provided for this discussion in my thesis. But for the time being, I shall like to indicate that, at this early stage in my research, there may be a connection between Hauerwas's reading of Kant, specifically on this issue of particularity, and Hauerwas's reliance upon Karl Barth's reading of Kant for this interpretation of Kant.

27 Hauerwas, *Peaceable Kingdom: A Primer in Christian Ethics* (Notre Dame, IN: University of Notre Dame Press, 1983), 18.

28 Hauerwas, *Peaceable Kingdom*, 10, citing Alasdair MacIntyre, *After Virtue* (Notre Dame: University of Notre Dame, 1981), 30.

29 Hauerwas and Burrell, "From System to Story," 158–90, passim.

defines humanity is the ability to make sound adjudications to regulate life. Life within the social and intellectual system this account creates, especially when it comes to issues connected to sexuality, seems to be ultimately about making good decisions, decisions we make while disjointed from particular covenants or habituated bodies.

Modern ethical discourse, according to Hauerwas, may be caricatured by suggesting all ethics begin by asking the same, mistimed question: What shall I do?[30] While Hauerwas agrees that seeking to determine appropriate actions is certainly pertinent for ethical inquiry, by locating the primal ethical question and, therefore, the essence of ethics in "action," modern ethicists betray reliance upon a particular perception of humanity.[31] In their view of humanity, the "I" of the individual is challenged to make autonomous decisions. Hauerwas maintains that this formulation of ethics and anthropology is characteristic of the descriptions prominent to the standard account.[32]

The standard narrative and its correlative anthropological commitments suggest that ethics is fundamentally about what Charles Taylor calls the "punctuated-self,"[33] who makes ethical determinations by rational adjudications through the execution of one's will. This focus upon decision-making limits ethics to a form of decisionism, which sees ethics primarily as the resolution of quandaries through right choices according to an internally deliberated, free execution of will by a rational agent detached from any particular constraints, such as time, place, or physical body. Thus, modern ethics, by relying upon this formulation of its leading question, unavoidably generates an ethical enterprise predicated upon decision-making as the purpose and function of morality and, in our case, sexual morality. More specifically for our purposes, this leads to a sexuality that can be and needs to be detached

---

30 Hauerwas, *Peaceable Kingdom*, 116; cf. Hauerwas, *Peaceable Kingdom*, 121–30, and Hauerwas and Burrell, "From System to Story," 163–68.

31 Hauerwas and Burrell, "From System to Story," 21.

32 Hauerwas and Burrell, 6–7.

33 I take this reading from Charles Taylor's *Sources of the Self: The Making of the Modern Identity.* (Cambridge, MA: Harvard University Press, 1992) It is defined essentially as the conception of the self, characterized by being "extentionless" and beyond external influence.

from particular sexual actions, that is, we can be something apart from doing something.

Decisionism is defined by two further distinguishing characteristics. These two characteristics are directly related to each other and pertain to anthropology. The first regards particularity, or rather the lack of it, while the second concerns a retreat inward into the mind of the self-agent.[34] This concentration upon the will as the locus of moral energies agglomerates those actions of the will into the practice of deciding. As such, ethics becomes nothing more than decisionism. Accordingly, the standard account's anthropology marches into plain view. The humanum has the capacity to will freely, and this capacity is predicated upon an internalized, rational, departicularized, disembodied nature. As a consequence, ethical conversations do not begin with our bodies but rather end with them. Bodies are only considered as objects to be regulated. Bodies and the actions of bodies are not recognized as fundamental to what it means to be human or part and parcel to being able to make rational determinations in the first place. Bodies and what bodies do should be the place where we begin our conversation as opposed to where we end them. To believe otherwise simply gives into the standard account and its associated anthropology, the humanum.

Introduced by Emmanuel Katongole in his text *Beyond Universal Reason*, *the humanum* is a term deployed by Katongole to refer to the modern idea of the independent, free, rational self as the origin and focus of all philosophical, theological, and ethical interests.[35] That is, the humanum is the form of persons anticipated by the standard account and illustrated well by Immanuel Kant. Kant's intellectual project—captured in the first quotation

---

34 For a more extensive discussion of particularity, see Hauerwas and Burrell's "From System to Story," 163ff. There, the authors consider how ethics became a decision-making procedure by detached, disembodied agents. For a more extensive discussion of the rise of interiority, see James McClendon, "From Decision to Story," in *From Christ to the World: Introductory Readings in Christian Ethics*, ed. Wayne Boulton et al. (Grand Rapids, MI: Eerdmans, 1994), 219ff. In his essay, McClendon identifies the need to order and the inability to do so sufficiently that prompts this change. Resultantly, the controlled will becomes synonymous with what it means to be human, allowing a new anthropology to emerge.

35 Emmanual Katongole, *Beyond Universal Reason: The Relation between Religion and Ethics in the Work of Stanley Hauerwas* (South Bend, IN: University of Notre Dame, 2000), 15.

above—describes his famed categorical imperative that integrates his ethics with his anthropology, that is, a person is most fundamentally understood as one who exercises will.[36] What gives persons their humanity is their ability to choose, and that definition of what it means to be human also underlies the church's doctrinal pronouncements on human sexuality.

The standard account's emerging anthropology may be seen in Kant's metaphysical distinctions, dividing the self between the inner and outer self. The inner self is free while the outer is conditioned, which he illustrates by his conceptualization of causality. Kant's notion of causality allows for a single direction of influence from the inner to the outer, which provides several consequences for his ethics.[37] Kant's true "self-in-itself" stands apart from activities. It affects the world but is not affected by the sensible world. This self is constitutive of the reasoning and willing activities of the mind.[38] Thus, Kant's methodology yields a dualistic conception of personhood that downgrades the body. Kant surmises:

> [We] have proved, beyond all question, that bodies are mere appearances of our outer sense and not things in themselves. We are therefore justified in saying that our thinking subject is not corporeal; in other words, that, inasmuch, as it is represented by us as object of inner sense, it cannot, in so far as it thinks, be an object of outer sense, that is, an appearance in space. This is equivalent to saying that thinking beings, *as such*, can never be found by us among outer appearances, and that their thoughts, consciousness, desires, etc., cannot be outwardly intuited. All these belong to inner sense.[39]

It has been my task to illustrate how the standard account assumes a particular type of person, the humanum. This standard story bespeaks a reality that consists of a series of binary oppositions, which necessarily includes

---

36 "I ought never to act except in such a way that I can also will that my maxim should become a universal law."

37 H. J. Paton, "Analysis of the Argument," in *Groundwork of the Metaphysic of Morals,* 47.

38 Howard Caygill, *A Kant Dictionary* (Hoboken, NJ: Wiley-Blackwell, 1995), 260.

39 Kant, *Critique of Pure Reason* (n.p.: Riga, 1781), 338–39. Cf. "But time and space, with all phenomena therein, are not in themselves things. They are nothing but representations and cannot exist out of and apart from the mind." Kant, *Critique of Pure Reason*, 339.

persons who are likewise bifurcated. This bifurcation isolates the punctuated (or delimited or clearly defined), inward self from the contingent, outward self. This punctuated self, identified from within a modern philosophical and theological tradition, must remain unattached to particularities. This being the case, autonomy and individualism are paramount descriptions of the humanum. This particular vision of the self generates an ethical project predicated upon decision-making as the identification and resolution of moral quandaries through the right execution of will. Such a vision of reality alters the degree to which ethical practices and habits are understood to impact who we ultimately are.

The *Eschaton Adam*, an Alternative to the Humanum

As I will hint at in my final section, the standard account's goal is for each individual self to see and to be the humanum, while conversely the gospel account seeks for us to see and become the *eschaton adam*. These anthropological visions hold dissimilar expectations, that is, persons are expected to be autonomous and individualistic as the humanum versus holy corporate and holy corporeal as the eschaton adam. These different expectations reshape our ethics and ethical praxis, producing these two different kinds of persons. As can be expected, such divergent anthropologies promote contrasting doctrinal priorities for the church.

In my estimation, the church has inappropriately and latently built its doctrine of human sexuality upon the humanum rather than the eschaton adam. For instance, descriptions like "homosexual" and "heterosexual" are not offered in a linguistic and conceptual vacuum. To name an action and to classify that action as appropriate or inappropriate, we must have the perceptive capacity to see that action and the conceptual structuring in which to place it. The root of perception and classification involves understanding how descriptions like "homosexual" and "heterosexual" acquire meaning. To understand better how all language acquires meaning, including descriptions like "homosexual" and "heterosexual," a look at George Lindbeck's works proves helpful.

In his exploration of how knowledge and understanding is formed, particularly church doctrine, Lindbeck arrives at what he feels is the preferred methodology for asserting a theological claim through what he terms the cultural-linguistic alternative.[40] In that alternative, first, liturgical practices and scripture are taken seriously as central components that are enacted when telling the church's narrative. The practices and stories of the church produce a distinctive knowledge and form a certain kind of person. And, second, this alternative allows for flexibility in the time and space the community needs as it shifts and reconsiders its narrative differently at different points and places and as told by different people. In other words, this model assumes particular places, practices, and bodies at the beginning of theological and ethical conversation. Therefore, claims grounded in a gospel narrative, rather than the standard narrative, have a distinctly different structure and character.[41]

The principal language and habits of the church—that is, the salvation narrative enacted in worship events—create a circle of interlocution, providing a hermeneutical framework. This circle produces for the worshiper the capacity to see the world as described and enacted by the worshiping community. This hermeneutical framework is Lindbeck's cultural-linguistic alternative.[42] Generally, this speaking/acting community establishes the framework necessary for perceiving reality, the world, and the self. Specifically, the

---

40 In Lindbeck's work *The Nature of Doctrine*, he outlines three typologies for epistemology: (1) cognitive-propositional, (2) experiential-expressive, (3) cultural-linguistic. The first two models rely upon an epistemological methodology that assumes a seeing prior to an ability to say what is seen. The last model, the one he and I are more reliant upon, relies upon a methodology of saying what something is and then being able to see it. George Lindbeck, *The Nature of Doctrine: Religion and Theology in a Postliberal Age* (Philadelphia: Westminster Press, 1984), 31–41.

41 Lindbeck, *The Nature of Doctrine*, 33. I specifically include a reference to George Lindbeck's work given the impact Lindbeck has upon Hauerwas and given the explicit attention paid to Lindbeck by Hauerwas in his own writings.

42 In Lindbeck's work, *The Nature of Doctrine*, he outlines three typologies for epistemology; (1) cognative-propostitional, (2) experiential-expressive, (3) cultural-linguistic. The first two models rely upon an epistemological methodology that assumes a seeing prior to an ability to say what is seen. The last model, the one he and I are more reliant upon, relies upon a methodology of saying what something is and then begin able to see it. George Lindbeck, The Nature of Doctrine: Religion and Theology in a Postliberal Age (Philadelphia: Westminster Press, 1984), 31–41.

particular narrative spoken and enacted—in this case, the Christian narrative of salvation—gives concrete substance to what is perceived.

An important point needs making. If narrative informs knowing, then the particular narrative told creates a particular known world. This includes what we know about what it means to be human. Thus, narrative and anthropology are linked, bolstering my critique of the denomination's statements on human sexuality. As already observed, the church affirms that sexuality is a good gift given to all persons and that persons are only fully who they are called to be after they have accepted that gift and had it affirmed by society and the church. This initial description, in and of itself, does not wholly identify the anthropology operative in the church's own statements on human sexuality but begins to suggest a fixed nature that is constitutive of what it means to be human, which includes the rejection of homosexual practice while simultaneously affirming the sacred worthiness of homosexuals.[43]

This ability to separate act (i.e., having homosexual sex) from the sacredness of being a homosexual person necessitates a latent commitment by the church to an anthropology where we can be homosexuals (or heterosexuals) without engaging in homosexual (or heterosexual) sex. If this were not the case, then the church would not be able to describe someone as fully human in his/her sexuality and concurrently deny any connection between that sexuality and sexual acts. Implicitly, act and being have been severed. Vitally, such a division of act from being would have significant consequences for the church's notion of sanctification and other seminal theological positions, if extrapolated across church doctrine. This division of the inner self from embodied action is emblematic of the humanum and representative of the kind of persons the modern ethical project requires. As described, in that formulation of humanity, articulated through the standard account, persons are understood to be independent, free, and rational selves.[44] This humanum is distinguished by a duality, a duality that has become the basis for the

---

43 *The Discipline, 2012*, ¶140, 101.

44 Katongole, *Beyond Universal Reason*, 15.

church when discussing human sexuality, that is, the inner self as gifted with a particular sexuality like homosexuality or heterosexuality and the outer self, which is defined by observable actions and negative or positive strictures.

Concluding Prescription: A Suggested Remedy

> "In God's self-revelation, Jesus Christ, we see the splendor of our true humanity."[45]

> Thus it is written, "The first man, Adam, became a living being"; the last Adam became a life-giving spirit.[46]

As I have intimated above, turning to the gospel account and the *eschaton adam* offers a profoundly different conceptualization of human sexuality and what constitutes commendable practices. Such an anthropology should be well grounded in a Christology defined by Incarnational narrative practices. We begin with Christ to craft our theological anthropology for two reasons. First, as the initial citation above confirms, Christ is the place where The UMC already begins. In its claims about the gracious life of Jesus Christ, the church intentionally includes an important anthropological description.

Randy Maddox, also, identifies this tendency to understand humanity christologically within John Wesley's own writings. And possibly even more important for our work, understanding humanity is not just christological but eschatological. In other words, Maddox identifies a tendency within Wesley to see Christ as revealing who we are meant to be prospectively rather than retrospectively. That means that Christ demonstrates for us who we are to become rather than to what we must return:

> The late Wesley decisively shifted the focus of his ultimate hope from "heaven above" to the future new creation. Indeed, the new creation became one of the most prominent themes of his late sermons. These sermons leave no doubt that the new creation will be a physical place, though each of its basic elements will be dramatically improved over present conditions. Indeed, they will be even better than the paradise

---

45 *The Discipline, 2016,* ¶102, 52.

46 1 Corinthians 15:45.

that Adam and Eve knew. There is also no doubt that all creatures will partake in the new creation. . . . For Wesley it was a quite serious matter of theodicy. He argues that the only satisfactory answer to questions that the present evil in the world raises about the wisdom and goodness of God is for God to restore in salvation even *more* than was present in original creation.[47]

Equally compelling for Maddox are the ethical consequences for Wesley's theology resulting from his prospective Christological anthropology. In Maddox's estimation, by committing to a concept of salvation deeply rooted in a progressive notion of "new creation," Wesley exchanges the heavenly metaphor of *rest* with one of new *life*. This exchange signals a conviction that eternal life entails a progressive transformation of the world and the self:

> [Wesley's] mature eschatology had been reshaped in keeping with his larger theological convictions and his orienting concern: the therapeutic grace of God was now truly universal (reaching all creation) and truly *responsible* (allowing for continual growth in responsiveness and transformation)![48]

This connection between Christology, anthropology, ethics, and transformation is vital to UM doctrine, as well as an expansive conceptualization of sanctification. However, there is a more compelling reason. That second reason originates with scripture.

In Paul's First Letter to the Corinthians, he describes the significance of the Resurrection. In describing this significance, Paul juxtaposes the sinful nature introduced by the first Adam with the alteration of that nature offered by the second Adam. This second Adam is the first fruits of God's eschatological recapitulation of humanity and all of creation. Paul says, "for as all die in Adam, so all will be made alive in Christ."[49] Later in that same chapter, Paul continues, "Thus it is written, 'The first man, Adam, became

---

47 Randy Maddox, *Responsible Grace: John Wesley's Practical Theology* (Nashville: Kingswood Books, 1994), 253.

48 Maddox, *Responsible Grace*, 253.

49 1 Corinthians 15:22.

a living being'; the last Adam became a life-giving spirit."[50] This risen Christ is representative of true humanity and the basis for our conceptualization of the *eschaton adam*.

Eschaton derives from the Greek *eschatos* (meaning last, final, or completion). *Adam* comes from the Hebrew word *adhām*, meaning humanity. Together, the new phrase eschaton adam[51] describes how Christ reveals the ultimate teleological purpose for what it means to be human. Thus, this climactic declaration by Paul in his First Letter to the Corinthians lays out for the church the beginnings of a Christocentric theological anthropology, that is, the eschaton adam. By taking Paul's motion together with Wesley and The UMC's as our starting points, we may illustrate a portrait of humanity derived from the gospel narrative.[52] This theological anthropology offers many salient characteristics of the eschaton adam. For our purpose, two of those characteristics—(1) corporateness and (2) corporeality—are important, as they imply a necessary notion of humanity that is both embodied through ritualistic practices and inherently relational in nature. In sum, sexuality with its assumed sexual practices and covenantal partnerships advance and deepen what it means to be human.

This reconceptualization resets our bodies within the church's larger theological imaginings and supplies the church with a different and distinct way to have these vital conversations. Ultimately, what results is, I hope, a consideration of human sexuality that is more about covenantal practices that form persons into the kind of people they are destined to be and/or become. These practices are inextricable from who we are, having the secondary and consequential effect of undercutting the often transactional or

---

50 1 Corinthians 15:45.

51 This notion of the eschaton adam, while found as a term in scripture, is an anthropological concept I am introducing, here, as a replacement for what I see as the disjointed anthropology of the humanum.

52 Importantly, the terms "gospel narrative" and "gospel account" are not phrases meant to limit the narrative of the church to the four Gospels. Rather, the terms "gospel narrative" or "gospel account" are used, here, in a more general sense, encompassing the entirety of the New Testament and early church witness. For this reason, the word "gospel" is spelled without using the capital "G," differentiating it from the formal names given to the four standard Gospels. This distinction will be maintained throughout this text.

transitory nature of our language and assumptions about human sexuality and those sexual practices that predominate—a sexual culture defined by notions like "hooking up," being "friends with benefits," and polyamory. In other words, these practices (habits) and our bodies are not separable or distinguishable services and commodities. We cannot disassociate ourselves from our bodies and from who we are meant to be. Thus, our bodies cannot be traded or regulated in any effective way that does not have consequential impact on who we fundamentally are.

As argued above, our denomination seems to have a theological problem expressed in doctrinal commitments that assume distinct anthropologies. When speaking about the issues of human sexuality, the church predicates its claims, in part, on the anthropology, that is, the humanum, presumed and produced by the standard account. Conversely, when speaking about sanctification and Christian perfection, the church does not rely on the standard account and does not project the humanum into doctrinal formulation. Quite the opposite, the church diligently relies upon the gospel account, projecting the eschaton adam into its doctrinal deliberations. As a result, the church is caught in a predicament: (1) hold on to two divergent, competing worldviews and their informative narratives and derivative anthropologies, or (2) select one narrative and one anthropology that can invite the church to rearticulate those parts of its doctrine that were predicated upon the narrative and anthropology it jettisoned. It seems the latter of these options is the only viable way forward for the church. If taken, the narrative embraced must be the gospel account. The coherence of this central story has specific anthropological and ethical consequences, particularly given the Incarnation—as the true expression of humanity—and the practice of the Eucharist—as elemental to what it means to be or embody Christ.

Moreover, if taken, this second option requires that the denomination rebuild its doctrine on human sexuality on a radically different notion of humanity. That new concept of humanity is the eschaton adam, a notion of the self that is (1) grounded in the central narrative and practices of the church, (2) wholly Incarnational (and Trinitarian) in character, and (3) comfortably insistent that habits affect and define who we are in fundamentally impactful ways. In other words, we are our habituated bodies. Bodies—their sexuality, gender, weaknesses, strengths, and complexity—are not dispensable or seen to be something principally best understood by Christian ethics as exterior objects to be regulated. Rather, bodies and the habits that form them and the stories that describe them are essential to who we are and our doctrinal claims. In such a rendering of who we are, the church's current claims tend to separate act from being, sexuality from sexual practice. This separation makes our sexual bodies incoherent.

Finally, if our notion of sexuality and sexual practices is rooted in an anthropology with its concomitant Incarnational story and Eucharistic practices, then our regulation of sexuality might be wholly reconsidered. If the church takes this alternative approach, it seems that our first discussion will never be what decisions need to be made about compatible or incompatible sexual practices but, rather, a discussion of what it means to be fundamentally corporate and corporeal and what habits might best advance persons toward their full humanity. This anthropology and recalibration of our conceptualizations will repair our bodies' unnatural dislocation from within our theological imaginations. Now, that feels better.

METHODISTS AND MUSLIMS
Better Together

Jon R. Powers
University Chaplain, Ohio Wesleyan University

> O mankind! We created
> You from a single (pair)
> Of a male and a female,
> And made you into
> Nations and tribes, that
> Ye may know each other
> (Not that ye may despise
> Each other). Verily
> The most honoured of you
> In the sight of Allah
> Is (he who is) the most
> Righteous of you.
> —The Holy Qur'an, Surah 49:13, Yusuf Ali
> translation

But I say to you that if you are angry with a brother or sister, you will be liable to judgment. . . . So when you are offering your gift at the altar, if you remember that your brother or sister has something against you, leave your gift there before the altar and go; first be reconciled to your brother or sister, and then come and offer your gift.

—Matthew 5:22-24, CEB

A big part of what the 21st century will be about is whether religion is

> a bubble of isolation,
> a barrier of division,
> a bomb of destruction or
> a bridge of cooperation.

Lots of leaders and movements have been pushing for

> the bubble,
> the barrier and
> the bomb,

and I think now you're starting to see

a critical mass of participants and leaders building bridges.

—Eboo Patel, Founder and President of Interfaith Youth Core

Ignorance Is Not Bliss

My ignorance about Muslims and all things Islam was an innocent result of my being born on the cold summer shores of Lake Michigan in Ludington, Michigan, sixty-seven years ago, third in the line of seven poor pig-farm boys, to an uneducated but brilliant Englishman father and an irascible and comparatively highly educated Swedish mother, and then raised through much of my childhood by an illiterate but wonderfully wise old woman who was a blood-blend of Oklahoma Chickasaw Indian and African American. My next-door neighbor, who was sometimes my Sunday School teacher, was a shrunken little man with beautiful long white hair who played the piano and occasionally had me and my brothers up to his house to sit straight-legged on his old horse-hair couch as we consumed milk and cookies while we listened appreciatively to him play and sing for us the songs that he had written. It was not until years later, when I saw him on national television as a guest on the Tennessee Ernie Ford Show, that I realized he was the famous author of the hymn "The Old Rugged Cross." I just knew him all those years as my gentle, loving neighbor, the Reverend George Bernard.

Yet, through all these many blessings of my formative years, there were no Muslims in my midst. So I did not know until decades later that, as a Methodist, Muslims were my scriptural and spiritual cousins. I did not gain that wonderful discovery until I became a United Methodist minister appointed to serve in church-related higher education.

Oh, These College Kids Today

In his afterword to Eboo Patel's brilliant book *Sacred Ground: Pluralism, Prejudice, and the Promise of America*, Martin Marty cites "Seven Deadly Sins of the college campus—ignorance, intolerance, apathy, unawareness, prejudice, distraction, and exclusiveness."[1] These maladies do not begin with college but are bred in the bones of our nation's predominant youth culture. The breeding ground is ferociously fertile: social media, music, movies, fashion, and peer pressure.

Yet the antithesis to such concerns is also bred in the bones of our youth themselves; we see it vibrantly expressed in the personal essays of high school youth as they apply to be enrolled at Ohio Wesleyan, where I serve. They speak of their transformative experiences from youth groups, church camps, mission teams, and community service. They yearn for an academic setting where they can explore their deepest passions without betraying their acute awareness of the world's great needs; where they can be their whole self— brain, body, soul—without being mocked or marginalized. They hunger for integrity, purpose, meaning—and more often than not, they hunger for a

---

1   Eboo Patel, *Sacred Ground: Pluralism, Prejudice, and the Promise of America* (Boston: Beacon Press, 2012), 170; for a related review of this crucial concern for campus ministry, see also David Kinnaman with Aly Hawkins, *You Lost Me: Why Young Christians Are Leaving Church . . . and Rethinking Faith* (Grand Rapids, MI: Baker, 2011).

place where they can find and celebrate coherence between their exploding environment and their traditional truths.

Martin Marty goes from listing his seven deadly maladies to proclaiming the good news that these are not the only seeds being planted in our nation today. The good news, reports Marty, is that many colleges and universities across the nation are "efficient and decisive locales for encountering and engaging the young" in matters of deep faith, character, and leadership development.[2]

The good news of this chapter is that, because of the attributes and passions of students as described here by Martin Marty, my students have taught me more about Islam than I ever dreamed I needed to know, and it has changed my mind, my heart, my soul, and the way I serve as a university chaplain and as a disciple of Jesus Christ.

Lessons My Students Taught Me

Over the past four decades as an ordained minister and campus chaplain in The United Methodist Church, I have learned, mostly from my students, what it means to love my neighbors who are Muslim; what it means that Islam and Christianity have more in common than in opposition; what it means to pray as a Christian in the middle of a thousand Muslim neighbors, kneeling reverently with them on a *masjid* carpet at a local mosque; what it means to read the Gospels of Jesus Christ with a Muslim student for his Ramadan devotions; and what it means to read the Qur'an with a Muslim student for my Lenten devotions.

One of my first encounters with a Muslim student was in my early years as the chaplain at Adrian College in Michigan. In my first conversation with him, he burst out with this indictment, "What's wrong with you Protestants, Chaplain, is that you do not respect the Holy Mother Mary like we Muslims and the Catholics do!" The ensuing in-depth conversation between us led to the formation of my first interfaith chaplaincy program. He and I formed

---

2   Patel, *Sacred Ground*, 170.

a weekly luncheon group we called "M&Ms"—Methodists and Muslims. We maintained an open-ended agenda: where did Methodists and Muslims differ; what did we hold in common? We discovered, over time, that Muslims and Methodists had more in common than we had in conflict. When I was appointed to Ohio Wesleyan as University Chaplain a few years later, I maintained this dialogue with a student group initially led by me and a small group of student leaders: a Muslim, Hindu, Catholic, Jew, and Protestant. We called our group Common Texts, and the group is now in its twentieth year. Our Common Texts topics are determined by the students from year to year but usually include such repeated topics as food and diet, gender roles, prayer practices, ideas and practices concerning body fluids, death and burial rituals, war and peace, and (of course) interfaith dating. It is not unusual for students in this not-for-academic-credit group to run off to the library after an intense conversation to find out more about their own faith's perspective on a particular topic. Some students also end up running with a topic from Common Texts for a class paper or even for their senior research topic.

Many other lessons have come to me from my students through unplanned and uncharted conversations. Early on in my years at Ohio Wesleyan, I found myself sitting with my student imam and his Hindu friend to discuss a new idea they had for butchering a goat on campus, and whether I could help them persuade the local health department to give us a special waiver for that holiday ritual (I did; they did; and we did). In the midst of this meeting, the Hindu student interrupted to ask me a question that apparently had been a topic of debate in his residence hall earlier that week. "How is it, Chaplain," he asked, "That you as a Christian can allow those of us who are Muslim or Hindu or Buddhist or Sikh or Jewish to pray in the chapel?"

Before I could answer, the Muslim student jumped up, pointed to the imposing painting of Jesus over my desk, and said in an enthusiastic voice, "It's because of him!" "What do you mean, because of him?" I asked the Hindu student with bewilderment. "Well, you know," responded the Muslim student imam, "When the Christians eat Jesus, they call him the Host! So if Chaplain is going to represent Jesus with integrity, he has to be hospitable!"

That marvelous exchange quickly led to a change in conversation from goat-slaughtering to Christian hospitality and much more. I learned quite a lot that day about the power of the incarnate Jesus as Host. I also learned about the power and potential of my witness as a disciple of Jesus Christ in the midst of interfaith conversation. I came to learn from such encounters that, if I want to engage in such interfaith conversations with Muslims and others, I better hone my knowledge of both my own faith and the faith of others. So coupled with my ordination commitment to maintain the intellectual rigors of the Oxford scholar-priest-evangelist John Wesley as best I could, the wisdom of William Shakespeare became like a mantra to me. "Ignorance is the curse of God; knowledge is the wing wherewith we fly to heaven."[3] If I wish to be relevant to my students in the twenty-first century, I need to learn more about the Muslims in our midst.

So What about the Muslims in Our Midst?

Like so many of his Jewish and Christian "cousins" before him in the legendary lineage of Abraham, Sarah, and Hagar, the Prophet Muhammad faced a cacophony of chaos that transformed him into a religious and political refugee. The consequent migration of Muhammad and his followers in the Hijra of 622 CE marked the beginning of what has been 1,394 years of contradictory and conflicting conditions for Muslims throughout the globe: dominance and displacement, imposition and dispossession, acclamation and marginalization.

Over the centuries, the contributing factors that led to the migration of Muslims were expansive, explosive, and sometimes contradictory—still religious and political, to be sure, but also geographical, militaristic, economic, linguistic, cultural, xenophobic, racial, and occasionally self-imposed. The consequences of these disruptions were often debilitating. Oppression,

---

3   William Shakespeare, *King Henry IV*, Second Part, Act 4, Scene 7 (New York: E. F. Dutton & Co., 1936), 76, lines 71–72. For a rollicking review of how "knowledge is the wing wherewith we fly to heaven," see Pastor Don Mackenzie, Rabbi Ted Falcon, and Sheikh Jamal R. Tahman, *Getting to the Heart of Interfaith: The Eye-Opening Hope-Filled Friendship of a Pastor, a Rabbi and a Sheikh* (Woodstock, VT: Skylight Paths, 2009).

suppression, repression, and depression were frequently experienced, and some consequences were severe: starvation, violence, and murder, even genocide.

According to United Nations spokesman Edwards Adrian, the United Nations High Commissioner for Refugees (UNHCR) reported in the summer of 2016 that population displacement greatly increased in numbers, causing dire consequences that negatively impacted communities and cultures throughout the globe. With the world population at 7.4 billion, one in every 113 persons is now either an asylum-seeker, internally displaced, or a refugee. Displacement totaled 65.3 million people. At no time since the UNHCR began keeping records has the cumulative impact of war, poverty, persecution, and political instability forced more people from their homes than now. Every 60 seconds in 2015, twenty-four more people were forced to flee; that is four times more than just a decade earlier, when only six people fled every 60 seconds. The vast majority of this historically high displacement was Muslim; the three countries that made up half the world's refugees in 2015 were all predominantly Muslim populations: Syria (4.9 million), Afghanistan (2.7 million), and Somalia (1.1 million).[4]

The United Nations High Commissioner for Refugees, Filippo Grandi, expressed this concern in vividly human terms. He reported that a major problem in the world today was that nativist impulses and xenophobic fears have led to some nations simply closing their borders and turning their backs on these displaced persons.

> At sea, a frightening number of refugees and migrants are dying each year; on land, people fleeing war are finding their way blocked by closed borders. Closing borders does not solve the problem. . . . The willingness of nations to work together not just for refugees but for the collective human interest is what's being tested today, and it's this spirit of unity that badly needs to prevail.[5]

---

4   Adrian Edwards, UNHCR, "Global Forced Displacement Hits Record High," June 20, 2016, http://www
.unhcr.org/en-us/news/latest/2016/6/5763b65a4/global-forced-displacement-hits-record-high.html.

5   Edwards, "Global Forced Displacement."

Among the many triggers that have led to such harsh responses to Muslim immigrants, particularly in Western cultures, is a growing phobia against Islam. A comprehensive Gallup report on the contemporary phobic response of western nations to displaced persons of the Muslim faith reveals a serious challenge to solutions suggested by the United Nations's refugee report. Gallup researchers and scholars reflect that "a phobia, according to the Merriam-Webster dictionary, is an exaggerated, usually inexplicable and illogical fear of a particular object, class of objects, or situation. In recent years, a specific phobia has gripped Western societies—Islamophobia. Researchers and policy groups define Islamophobia in differing detail, but the term's essence is essentially the same, no matter the source: an exaggerated fear, hatred, and hostility toward Islam and Muslims that is perpetuated by negative stereotypes resulting in bias, discrimination, and the marginalization and exclusion of Muslims from social, political, and civic life."[6]

America's Myopic Response to Our Muslim Neighbors

Gallup reported that this disrespect, mistreatment, and intolerance of Muslims was a global phenomenon, but that the United States of America was among those countries that ranked highest in the world in terms of prejudice against Muslims, and that "religion and culture outpace politics . . . as the root cause of tension between Muslim and Western worlds. . . . Political interests can vary and change while cultural and religious differences are more ingrained within populations."[7]

In June 2016, the Southern Poverty Law Center undergirded the Gal-

---

6   Gallup, *Islamophobia: Understanding Anti-Muslim Sentiment in the West* (Washington, DC: Gallup World Headquarters, 2016), 1, http://www.gallup.com/poll/157082/islamophobia-understanding -anti-muslim-sentiment-west.aspx.

7   Gallup, 1. Islamophobia in America is often linked in the minds of many citizens to their fear of terrorism, and you may well have to confront the issues of terrorism before you can proceed to a calmer conversation about other Christian-Muslim matters. For further study of terrorism in relation to American Islamophobia, I recommend Ken Ballen, *Terrorists in Love: The Real Lives of Islamic Radicals* (New York: Free Press, 2011); Norman Daniel, *Islam and the West: The Making of an Image*, rev. ed. (Oxford: One World, 1993); Fawaz A. Gerges, *Journey of the Jihadist: Inside Muslim Militancy* (Orlando: Harcourt, 2006); Charles A. Kimball, *Religion, Politics, and Oil: The Volatile Mix in the Middle East* (Nashville: Abington Press, 1992); Bernard Lewis, *What Went Wrong? Western Impact and Middle*

lup's reflections by documenting an alarming increase in the number of American-based hate groups since 2000. This rise exploded in 2009 when Barack Hussein Obama assumed the office of president of the United States, then leveled off and declined slightly again in 2011. However, in 2015, these American-grounded hate groups rose to a near all-time high of 892.[8]

Of greatest concern is the fact that America's anti-Muslim hate groups in particular have increased the most—42 percent between 2014 and 2016. Each of these anti-Muslim hate groups represent, in varying degrees, an intense blend of religious bigotry, political hostility, threats of physical (and sometimes lethal) violence, and each vehemently challenges Islam's legitimate role as a respectable and acceptable religion.

To be sure, the terrorist attack on the World Trade Center on September 11, 2001, marked the chronological trigger for many of these anti-Muslim hate groups, but there is clear historical documentation of prior anti-Muslim movements that were religiously based, denying the legitimacy of Islam as a religion in America. Even so, the Southern Poverty Law Center reports that the more recent increase in the number of anti-Muslim hate groups is accompanied by a greater intensity in the phobic dimension of a cultural and religious reaction to Islam itself and to *shari'a* law in particular. The Southern Poverty Law Center has documented the consistent and intense hostility of these groups toward Muslims in America. These organizations depict their Muslim neighbors as fundamentally alien with an inherent set of negative traits. They believe that their Muslim neighbors are: irrational; intolerant; violent; promoters of pedophilia, marital rape, and child marriage; evil; without basic human values; culturally inferior; sexually aberrant; unclean and unkempt; and vile enemies of Christianity and everything else Americans hold dear. These anti-Muslim hate groups in America seem obsessed with conspiratorial constructs of fearful fantasies that: their Muslim-American

---

Eastern Response (Oxford: University Press, 2002); Bernard Lewis, *The Crisis of Islam: Holy War and Unholy Terror* (New York: The Modern Library, 2003).

8 "Hate Map" (poster) (Montgomery, AL: Southern Poverty Law Center, 2016), https://www.splcenter .org/fighting-hate/intelligence-report/2016/active-hate-groups-united-states-2015.

neighbors are inherently dangerous to the very foundation of America; their Muslim neighbors are secretly organized to surreptitiously undermine and then replace the institutions of our American democracy and the United States Constitution with shari'a law; and they ultimately want to destroy all institutions of Western civilization with oppressive and absolute Islamic rule. Much of this conspiratorial myopia and hate-infested fear is anchored in theological confusion about Islam and American Muslim culture generally, and shari'a law in particular.

Over the past decade, these American-based anti-Muslim hate groups were notably influential in the majority of state legislative actions to outlaw shari'a law. Large segments of proposed legislation were lifted verbatim from these anti-Muslim organizations and formed a distinct pattern of collaboration from state to state.[9]

The intense effort to disparage and destroy Islamic culture in America is not limited to these anti-Muslim hate groups. Indeed, America's mainstream political institutions have begun to play a key role in the oppression and suppression of American Islamic culture.

Increasingly, a critical vortex for American Islamophobia has been American presidential politics. In 2014, former United States Speaker of the House Newt Gingrich insisted that Muslim Americans were like Nazis who sought to infiltrate American culture in the last century; Muslims, he alleged, were trying to do the same thing to America in the twenty-first century. He proclaimed, "*Shari'a* is a mortal threat to the survival of freedom in the United States."[10] He also demanded, "We should frankly test every person here who is of a Muslim background, and if they believe in *Shari'a*, they should be de-

---

9   Christopher Bail, *Terrified: How Anti-Muslim Fringe Organizations Become Mainstream* (Princeton: Princeton University Press, 2015), 103ff.

10   The Bridge Initiative Group, "Islamophobia in the 2016 Elections," April 25, 2015; updated June 2016, http://bridge.georgetown.edu/islamophobia-and-the-2016-elections/. See also http://bridge .georgetown.edu/tag/2016-election, and http://bridge.georgetown.edu/when-islamophobia-turns -violent-the-2016-u-s-presidential-elections/. For a good comparative review of how America has treated major religious immigrant groups historically, I recommend John L. Esposito, Yvonne Haddad, and Jane Smith, *Immigrant Faiths: Christians, Jews, and Muslims Becoming Americans* (Walnut Creek, CA: AltaMira Press, 2002).

ported."[11] Another presidential candidate, Dr. Ben Carson, avowed that he would not appoint a Muslim to his cabinet or as a federal judge; he shared fervently Mr. Gingrich's contempt for shari'a law, affirming that there was a "creeping attempt . . . to gradually ease shari'a law and the Muslim faith into our government."[12]

The rhetoric of the 2016 presidential campaign raised the specter of Islamophobia to a fever pitch. Senator Lindsay Graham of South Carolina stated that the racially-obsessed young white man who shot his black Christian hosts in cold blood while attending a prayer and Bible study session with them at an African American Episcopal Church in Charleston was a direct reflection of "Mideast hate" (read: Muslim hate). Former Pennsylvania Senator Rick Santorum charged both Presidents Bush and Obama with giving "all Muslims a pass for identifying a cancer within their own body." Texas Senator Ted Cruz declared that shari'a law in America is an "enormous problem." Senator Rand Paul of Kentucky announced that the Muslim worshipers who sought to establish their Islamic community center a few blocks from the World Trade Center demonstrated motives akin to the Ku Klux Klan. Former Arkansas Governor Michael Huckabee, who also is an ordained Christian minister, declared that Islam "promotes the most murderous mayhem on the planet" ("Islamophobia").

Throughout the American Presidential campaign in 2015–2016, incidents of violence against Muslims in America increased at an alarming rate. Mosques have been vandalized since with "Jesus Graffiti" painted on the walls of the prayer center; other Muslim communities have been blocked by local protesters from building mosques in their own communities; random Muslim cab drivers and shopkeepers have been killed in documented hate crimes; and sometimes Sikhs, who are not Muslim, have been identified mistakenly by shooters as Muslim. Muslims at prayer in their neighborhood

---

11 Hrafnkell Haraldsson, "Gingrich Goes Full-Tilt Crazy With Plan to Test Every Muslim in America," Politicus USA, July 15, 2016, http://www.politicususa.com/ 2016/07/15/gingrich-full-tilt-crazy-test-muslim -america.html.

12 The Bridge Initiative Group, "Islamophobia."

mosques have been bombed, shot, and threatened by armed, open-carry, gun-toting protesters ("Islamophobia").

Also during the American Presidential campaign of 2015–2016, the nominee of the Republican Party, Donald Trump, called for "a total and complete shutdown of all Muslims entering the United States."[13] Trump and at least two other presidential candidates promoted various forms of undercover police surveillance of local neighborhood mosques to expose allegedly suspicious terrorist threats, and even proposed to shut down selected mosques if they felt the mosques were ideologically or theologically unacceptable. Trump repeatedly shouted at massive rallies that "Islam hates us!" and repeatedly recited a debunked myth that US Gen. John Pershing had executed Muslim prisoners in the Philippines with bullets he had dipped in pig's blood just to "show them."[14]

At one campaign rally, an unnamed supporter of Mr. Trump posed this question: "We have a problem in this country. It's called Muslims. We know our president is one. You know he's not even an American. We have training camps growing when [sic] they want to kill us. My question: When can we get rid of them?" Yet without a moment's hesitation, Mr. Trump replied: "We are going to be looking at that. We are going to be looking at a lot of different things" ("Islamophobia"). Months later, at yet another campaign town hall meeting, an unidentified citizen in the audience asked Mr. Trump, "Why aren't we putting our military retirees on that border or in TSA? Get rid of all these *heebee-jabees* they wear at TSA?"[15] (This was an apparent reference to the *hijab*, a head scarf worn by some Muslim women. Many young Muslim women with whom I serve as a University Chaplain in the Midwest wear the *hijab* as a personal preference to publicly affirm their spiritual devotion to God). Mr. Trump responded to the questioner, again without

13 Jenna Johnson, "Trump Calls for 'Total and Complete Shutdown of Muslims Entering the United States,'" *Washington Post*, Dec. 7, 2015.

14 The Bridge Initiative Group, "Islamophobia."

15 Alexandra Jaffe, "Trump Faces Question about Muslim 'Heebeejabees' at Town Hall," NBC News, Politics website, July 1, 2016, http://www.nbcnews.com/politics/2016-election/trump-faces-wild-questions -n-h-town-hall-n602056.

correction or hesitation, "I understand. . . . You know, and we are looking at that. . . . And we are looking at that. We're looking at a lot of things."[16]

Shari'a Law as a Convenient Scapegoat

Given these stunning illustrations of Islamophobia in American culture, it is evident that there are many dimensions to anti-Muslim sentiments. Yet a wide-spread fear of shari'a law serves as a core and convenient mortar connecting the rhetorical bricks of American Islamophobia. It also appears that far too many American political leaders are exploiting such phobic phenomena. It is not enough to acknowledge that there has never been, nor is there now, any effort anywhere in America for shari'a law to infiltrate local, state, regional, or national legislative processes, much less supersede in any way the Constitution of the United States of America.[17]

> Across the country, state legislators are considering proposed laws that would limit the ability of courts to adjudicate lawsuits brought by Muslims. Proponents of these measures argue that they are necessary because so-called "Shari'a law" is somehow taking over our courts. These claims are, simply put, wrong. They are based both on misinformation and a misunderstanding of how our judicial system works. There is no evidence that Islamic law is encroaching on our courts. On the contrary, the court cases cited by anti-Muslim groups as purportedly illustrative of this problem actually show the opposite: Courts treat lawsuits that are brought by Muslims or that address the Islamic faith in the same way that they deal with similar claims brought by people of other faiths or that involve no religion at all. These cases also show that sufficient protections already exist in our legal system to ensure that courts do not become impermissibly entangled with

16 Jaffe, "Trump Faces Question." For a closer examination of veil issues, I recommend: Katherine Bullock, *Rethinking Muslim Women and the Veil: Challenging Historical & Modern Stereotypes* (Herndon, VA: International Institute of Islamic Thought, 2003); Shelina Zahra Janmohamed, *Love in a Headscarf* (Boston: Beacon Press, 2010); Transcultural Educational Center and Ifta Office, Washington DC, *Seeing Through the Veil: Wearing the Veil in America* (McLean, VA: Transcultural Education Center, undated brochure); Amina Wadud, *Qur'an and Woman: Reading the Sacred Text from a Woman's Perspective* (New York: Oxford University Press, 1999).

17 American Civil Liberties Union, "Nothing to Fear: Debunking the Mythical "Shari'a Threat" to Our Judicial System," May 2011, 1.

religion or improperly consider, defer to, or apply religious law where it would violate basic principles of U.S. or state public policy.[18]

In a similar response to America's political penchant to deprecate Islam in general and shari'a law in particular, *USA Today* reporter Oliver Thomas observed, "Outlaw shari'a and you've outlawed 5 million to 8 million Americans."[19] Thomas went on to say,

> Iconic poet Carl Sandburg once was asked what was the dirtiest word in the English language. His answer might have surprised some people: Exclusive. The tendency to exclude others — to prejudge and ostracize — has dogged humankind and the United States since its inception. The first Jews to arrive in New York, then called New Amsterdam, were refused the right even to get off their ship. When Gov. Peter Stuyvesant's Dutch sponsors prevailed upon him to grant the Jews admission, they still weren't allowed to vote, hold office or serve in the militia. Throughout America's rich history of welcoming "your huddled masses," this dark thread of bigotry has marred our national tapestry. First, it was Jews, then blacks, Catholics, gays, and now, Muslims who must sometimes bear the brunt of our prejudices.[20]

Such thoughtful rebuttals to the increasingly irrational and myopic rendering of shari'a law are encouraging. At stake is the well-being of Muslim individuals, Muslim neighbors, and Muslim communities throughout America. Yet also at stake are our historical American values as a welcoming, inclusive, and wholesome culture.

At his first inaugural address, President Barack Hussein Obama reaffirmed this powerful vision of our American ideals.

> For we know that our patchwork heritage is a strength, not a weakness. We are a nation of Christians and Muslims, Jews and Hindus,

---

18 American Civil Liberties Union, "Nothing to Fear."

19 Oliver Thomas, "States Cracking Down on the Islamic Law Misunderstand the Right to Freedom of Religion," *USA Today*, December 11, 2012, http://www.usatoday.com/story/opinion/2012/12/11 /sharia-law-christians-muslims/1762143/. See also Noah Feldman, "What Shariah IS (and Isn't)," *New York Times*, Sunday, July 17, 2016, p. 48, where he makes a compelling argument that the American cultural, political, and legal attacks against Shari'a law are "rife with error."

20 Thomas, "States Cracking Down."

and non-believers. We are shaped by every language and culture, drawn from every end of this Earth; and because we have tasted the bitter swill of civil war and segregation, and emerged from that dark chapter stronger and more united, we cannot help but believe that the old hatreds shall someday pass; that the lines of tribe shall soon dissolve; that as the world grows smaller, our common humanity shall reveal itself; and that America must play its role in ushering in a new era of peace. To the Muslim world, we seek a new way forward, based on mutual interest and mutual respect.[21]

We now face a challenge, as Americans, as Christians, and as Methodist citizens in a global society. Shall we envision, engage, and act on this ideal of America as a nation of strength, inclusivity, and civility?

A Muslim-Methodist Bridge: Shari'a Law, *Usul al-Fiqh* and the Wesleyan Quadrilateral

So how might we responsibly and faithfully address this growing problem of Islamophobia in general and the defamation of shari'a law in particular?

I would suggest that the core question for us as Christians and as United Methodists may well be found in the now somewhat worn mantra: "What Would Jesus Do?" Yet, as a university chaplain who deals daily with crucial questions brought to me from the crucibles of college life and students' developmental crises, I would take that query a step further to ask, "What is God's will, and how might we best discern the will of God in this particular matter? What might we safely and confidently say about God's heart and mind in relation to Muslims and shari'a law? How might our sense of God's will in this matter inform our Christian beliefs and actions, including our roles as university and college chaplains and campus ministers?"

In my pursuit of greater understanding of this question, I have been blessed to begin a consultative and professional friendship with an American attorney in Columbus, Ohio. His name is Omar Tarazi. He is learned in American jurisprudence, shari'a law, and *usul al-fiqh* (Islamic jurisprudence). He

---

21 Barack Hussein Obama, First Inaugural Address, The White House, January 21, 2009, https://www .whitehouse.gov/blog/2009/01/21/president-barack-obamas-inaugural-address.

has published an extensive series of essays on law, economics, religion, and politics related to the United States Constitution and Supreme Court rulings since 1789.[22] He also has translated much of the Qur'an into approachable, colloquial poetry and prose.[23] From Mr. Tarazi, I have been solidly confirmed in my understanding that, contrary to the shrill myopic utterings of contemporary American Christians, politicians, and legislators, shari'a law is not an established legal code. Rather, shari'a law is a fluid concept, subject to a wide range of interpretations and applications that vary extensively and significantly depending upon the cultural, political, and economic context; the geographical region and country; and the particular sect of Islam being referenced at any given moment in history. To point to any specific point of shari'a law is a complex, delicate, and nuanced exercise. It is, perhaps, somewhat like trying to delineate a specific chess move on a kaleidoscopic, three-dimensional chess board, and declaring that, "There! This is the definition of what chess is all about."

So to speak of any specific application of shari'a law in America is comparable to asking about a specific application of Christian theology in America: to which particular Christian sect, in what particular region of the country, and at what particular moment in history are you directing your concern? There are, for instance, 7,183,193 United Methodists in the United States, which is only 0.02 percent of all Americans.[24] Yet within this small but often influential subgroup of American religious culture, there are a plethora of divisions, dissensions, and disruptive disputes about many aspects of what it means to live as a Methodist in America today, and if you point to any particular time in American history, you will discover that it was never any different than today; only the topics of dispute have changed from generation to generation.[25]

Even so, in both Methodism and Islam, there is a generally agreed upon

22 Omar Tarazi, *Omar Tarazi Esq. Blog*, Columbus, Ohio, 2009–2016, http://otarazi.blogspot.com.

23 Tarazi, https://plainenglishquran.com/.

24 See http://www.umc.org/gcfa/data-services and http://www.census.gov/popclock.

25 See http://www.umc.org/who-we-are/history.

process of discernment that links us as what I call theological cousins. I would venture that there is no formula more respected or more useful in Methodism than the construct which has been known in recent decades as the Wesleyan Quadrilateral. The beloved United Methodist scholar, Dr. Albert Outler, formulated the construct of the Wesleyan Quadrilateral as one of the *magnum opi* of his lifelong scholarly research and reflection on Wesley's life history and massive theological tomes. Outler synthesized the theological discernment processes of Wesley into four basic pillars: Scripture, Tradition, Experience, and Reason. *The Book of Discipline of The United Methodist Church* in recent decades has reaffirmed this discernment process as core to Methodism.[26] Our Christian faith is divinely revealed through each of these pillars:

- **Scripture.** We are, together with our Jewish and Muslim kin, "People of the Book." For us, this means the Old and New Testaments.[27] In addition to these sacred Judeo-Christian texts, some (including myself) also learn increasingly about our sacred heritage and God's revelations from the Qur'an, even though that is not yet common to all of us and may never be so.

- **Tradition.** We as Methodists are also anchored in the vast and diverse history and doctrines of Christianity developed over the past two millennia. For some of us (including me), this also includes our traditional relations both peaceful and violent over the past 1,300 years with our Muslim kin. Yet, again, that is not common to us all.

- **Experience.** We affirm that our theological discernment is dependent upon, made alive by, and becomes relevant through our personal and communal experiences, including our experiential encounters with our Jewish and Muslim kin.

---

26 "Our Theological Task," *The Book of Discipline of The United Methodist Church, 2012* (Nashville, TN: The United Methodist Publishing House, 2012), ¶105, 78–89.

27 The Old Testament is also called the Hebrew Bible.

🔶 **Reason.** Our individual and communal intellectual assessments, debates, analyses, and reflections, including for some of us our study and contemplation of Jewish and Islamic literature and theology, confirms and seals our process of theological discernments.

The good but perhaps challenging news is that these profound constructs of faith and life discernment we call the Wesleyan Quadrilateral are distinctly parallel to the profound constructs of faith and life discernment that comprise shari'a law and its undergirding principles of Islamic jurisprudence (*usul al-fiqh*, the human interpretation of the law of shari'a). Shari'a law is closely composed of and thoroughly grounded in the sacred texts of Islam, particularly the core scripture, the Qur'an, which is understood by Muslims to be the divine law of God revealed to the Prophet Muhammad. The Qur'an includes many references, quotations, and paraphrases from the sacred texts of both Judaism and Christianity.

Scripture as a Bridge

What might it mean for us, as Christians, that shari'a law and usul al-fiqh are based on Islamic scripture, which contains a massive amount of Judeo-Christian sacred texts? As a Christian minister, I proclaim the Gospel of Jesus Christ; I seek to live a life that gives witness to Jesus Christ as my Lord and Savior; and I strive to build bridges between Christianity and Islam. This is not antithetical to Christianity; it is a core teaching of Jesus. It is the embrace of the Samaritan as my neighbor; it is the intimate, intense, and redemptive conversation between Jesus and the woman at the well.

I include texts from the Qur'an in my personal faith study and in my Christian ministry, because the Qur'an tells us a lot of wonderful things about Jesus. For example, the Qur'an teaches Muslims to believe in Jesus, love Jesus, and honor Jesus. In fact, a Muslim cannot be a follower of the Qur'an unless he or she does believe in Jesus.[28]

Among the nearly one hundred references to Jesus in the Qur'an, the

---

28 Albeit as a prophet and not the divine Son of God.

Qur'an declares that Jesus was born of a virgin; Jesus spoke while he was still only a baby; Jesus healed the blind and the leper by God's leave; Jesus raised the dead by God's leave; Jesus is the Lord, the Christ, and the Messiah; Jesus is a Word from God, and a Holy Spirit from God; Jesus is honored in this world and in the hereafter; and Jesus is one of those brought nearest to God. Indeed, the only Judeo-Christian person who is referenced more often than Jesus in the Qur'an is a woman named Mary, the Holy Mother of Jesus.

In Genesis 21:15-19, God said to Hagar, the mother of Islam's forbearer Ishmael, "Don't be afraid. God has heard the boy's cry in this plight of his. Arise, lift up the boy, and hold him by the hand, for I will make of him a great nation." In the tenth chapter of the Gospel of John, it is written: "Jesus said, I have other sheep that do not belong to this fold. I must lead them, also, and they shall hear my voice. There shall be one flock then, one shepherd." We can begin to see that Christianity and Islam have a whole lot of common connections that we might want to explore in civil conversation with each other.

Is that even possible? Probably not with some folk. The Christian author of *The Biblical Year of Womanhood*, Rachel Held Evans, suggests that there are people who read their holy texts with "selective literalism." She writes, "Everyone's a Biblical literalist until you bring up gluttony . . . or divorce, or gossip, or slavery, or head coverings, or Jesus' teachings on nonviolence, or the 'abomination' of eating shellfish and the hell-worthy sin of calling other people idiots. Then we need a little context. Then we need a little grace. Then we need a little room to disagree."[29]

Some Christians will insist that Deuteronomy 5:1-22 (the Ten Commandments) is so sacred that it must be posted even in government buildings; yet many of these same people insist that the verses that follow (for instance, Deuteronomy 21:18-21—that rebellious children must be stoned to death) no longer apply to us.

------

29 Rachel Held Evans, "Everyone's a Biblical Literalist Until You Bring Up Gluttony," July 8, 2013, http://rachelheldevans.com/blog/literalist-gluttony.

Some Muslims, who are recognized within their own communities as "selective literalists" about the Qur'an, make similar judgments. However, in my experience as a Christian minister serving mostly as a university chaplain, the vast majority of American Muslims reflect the soul and substance of my friend and colleague, Dr. Eboo Patel. He is the founder and president of the nationally renowned Interfaith Youth Core, and he served as an interfaith advisor to President Barack Hussein Obama. Dr. Patel proclaims, "A big part of what the 21st century will be about is whether religion is a bubble of isolation, a barrier of division, a bomb of destruction, or a bridge of cooperation. Lots of leaders have been pushing for the bubble, the barrier, and the bomb. I think now you're starting to see a critical mass of participants and leaders building bridges."[30]

Tradition as a Bridge

What might it mean for us, as Christians, that shari'a law and usul al-fiqh are based on tradition? Here are the conceptual and operational parallels that seem most relevant: Core portions of both shari'a law and Islamic jurisprudence (usul al-fiqh) are based upon a sacred secondary source known as the Sunnah, which literally means "the well-known path" or the "well-trodden path." This can mean a literal path or practices of a person or culture that represent its traditional ways of thinking and acting. It most closely references rituals of worship, but it also refers to the variously recorded words, acts, and approvals of the Prophet and those who have transmitted those teachings over the centuries.[31] As with both Methodist doctrinal documents

---

30 Eboo Patel, "Look to Young People for Leadership in Interfaith Cooperation," Faith and Leadership Blog, October 10, 2011, 1.

31 Imran Ahsan Khan Nyazee, *Islamic Jurisprudence (Usul al-Fiqh)* (Selangor, Malasia: The Other Press, The International Institute of Islamic Thought, 2000), 162–69. For a deeper read on the various nuances of Shari'a law and usul al-fiqh as surveyed here, I recommend: Muhammad Baqir As-Sadr, *Lessons in Islamic Jurisprudence*, trans. Roy Parviz Mottahedeh (Oxford: One World Publications, 2003); Sadakat Kadri, *Heaven on Earth: A Journey Through Shari'a Law from the Deserts of Ancient Arabia to the Streets of the Modern Muslim World* (New York: Farrar, Straus and Giroux, 2012); Mohammad Hashim Kamali, *Principles of Islamic Jurisprudence*, 3rd ed. (Cambridge, UK: Islamic Texts Society, 2003); Mohammad Hashim Kamali, *Shari'ah Law: An Introduction* (Oxford: Oneworld, 2008).

and American constitutional law and jurisprudence, Sunnah has deepened and expanded over the centuries to include many intricate and complex nuances. This sense of respect for and dependence upon tradition in shari'a law and usul al-fiqh is reflected in the concept and practice of ijma', which literally means both "to determine" and more important "to agree upon." There are seven conditions which must be met for an ijma usul al-fiqh to be legally agreed upon. Just as such dynamics of discernment vary extensively within historical and contemporary Christianity, each of these steps within ijma' contains a complex diversity within Islam, depending upon particular local histories, cultures, and national constrictions. Even so, these are the basic steps of ijma'.

(1) It must be the consensus of those who have risen to the communal status of a jurist. (For those of us in the American Methodist tradition, that would be the members of the Judicial Council of The United Methodist Church; in secular America, that would be a judge or a panel of judges within any variety of levels of judicial rank and status.)

(2) It must be unanimous among all the judges involved (no split decisions as we have in Methodist and American jurisprudence).

(3) All the jurists must be of the people of Muhammad (as in American Methodism we do not allow Baptists or Presbyterians to rule on matters related to the United Methodist *Book of Discipline*).

(4) The consensus must have taken place after the death of the Prophet Muhammad, as anything discerned by the Prophet during his lifetime would be "settled law" already and need no further consensus.

(5) The agreement must be among the jurists of a single determined period (similar to the understanding in Methodism that each General Conference rules for the church for that particular quadrennial only; in American jurisprudence, each Congressional or Supreme Court session stands on its own merit, and only those serving in that session may vote in that session).

(6) The agreements must be related to matters of legal concern, not extrajudicial concerns like grammar, artistic tastes, or more general concerns

like ideas about the creation of the universe. (Don't even try to touch that one in terms of Methodism or American jurisprudence.)

(7) The ijma' must be compatible with Sunnah; the judicial consensus must faithfully reflect the core principles of the Qur'an. (For Methodism, this would be the core principles of the Gospels and Wesleyan theology as understood and deliberated through the centuries; within American jurisprudence, this would be the high respect of the courts for prior judicial judgments.)[32]

Experience as a Bridge

What might it mean for us, as Christians, that shari'a law and usul al-fiqh are based on experience? Within the function of shari'a law and usul al-fiqh, the concept of experience is embedded in the principle of *taqlid*, what we in American jurisprudence might call "case law," or, in contemporary Christian discernment, "What Would Jesus Do?" In practical, daily experience, *taqlid* might include such permissible legal discernments as a Muslim layperson accepting the opinion of a doctor; the opinion of a realtor in the valuation of property; the opinion of a butcher that the meat about to be purchased is *halal* (slaughtered according to Islamic ritual law); or even trusting the word of a child who relays permission to a guest that the guest is allowed to enter the home. Experiential value is not easily accepted by the most traditional of Islamic jurists, but it appears increasingly normative in contemporary Muslim culture.[33]

Reason as a Bridge

What might it mean for us, as Christians, that shari'a law and usul al-fiqh are based on reason? In the processes of shari'a law and usul al-fiqh, the concept and function of reason are absolutely fundamental, particularly in the principles of *qiyas* (analogy), *maslahah mursalah* (extended analogy), and *ijtihad* (interpretation). These terms, taken together, literally mean to mea-

---

32 Gerges, *Journey*, 182–85.

33 Gerges, 327–34.

sure or estimate one thing in terms of another, or to make two things equal by comparing each to the other, or to make a rational discernment through the process of comparative analysis and faithful reflection.[34] In Christianity, such a system of thought enabled Jesus to ask Rabbinic questions, such as, "Is man made for the Sabbath or is the Sabbath made for man?" or "Who among these—the lawyer, the priest, or the Samaritan—acted as the one who loved his neighbor?"

These examples are but a wee speck of the broader and deeper landscape of shari'a law and usul al-fiqh as these principles and practices have operated over many centuries. None of these principles are hard and fast in all of Islam; each concept and practice has evolved slowly and thoughtfully over time; each has shifted in widely diverse and particular ways in response to the cultural needs and demands of various locations and generations. Even so, it is clear that in shari'a law and usul al-fiqh, as in the Wesleyan Quadrilateral, *scripture* is and likely always will be primary; *tradition* is and likely always will be vital; and *experience* and *reason* are and likely always will be the dynamic principles that enable contemporary relevance and value for each generation, no matter where they may find themselves placed on this earth.

This brief review of the theological construct and context of shari'a law and usul al-fiqh holds significant implications for how Christian Americans might better relate to their Muslim neighbors. Many nuances of difference between shari'a law, usul al-fiqh, and the United States Constitution remain, mostly in the same way that some details within *The Book of Discipline of The United Methodist Church* do not comport in every nuance with state laws, national legislation, or the United States Constitution. For instance, the United States Supreme Court ruling on the constitutionality of same-sex marriage radically changed what was thought to be settled law in America. The majority opinion, written by Justice Anthony Kennedy, included these pivotal words, "The limitation of marriage to opposite-sex couples may long have seemed natural and just, but its inconsistency with the central meaning

---

34 Gerges, 213–323.

of the fundamental right to marry is now manifest."[35] Even so, *The Book of Discipline of The United Methodist Church* remains clearly opposed to same-sex marriage, and the debate (within both the church and the nation) remains unsettled. The bulk of such differences, however, are miniscule in relation to the core principles and practices that bind both our church and our nation in common cause.

The renowned English barrister and New York attorney Sadakat Kadri provides us with a clear and cleansing understanding of the ultimate impact of shari'a law and usul al-fiqh on American institutions now and in the future. He writes,

> The aspirational appeal of the *shari'a* has a significance that . . . has particular resonance in the United States. . . . The overwhelming majority of immigrants to the West have made their peace with secularism, and the remedies they expect from Islamic law are correspondingly minimal. A woman whose husband has abandoned her without speaking the words of release required by the *Qur'an* might approach a *mufti* (a Muslim religious authority comparable to a priest, pastor, or rabbi) in search of an annulment. Senior figures in a community will pay visits to the homes of disruptive teenagers to remind them of their religious roots. Muslims who are prudent as well as pious might ask scholars to tell them which mortgage and insurance products are consistent with Islamic jurisprudence. Every faith community in the United States, from the Amish to the Zoroastrians, has equivalent ways of doing right by God. The only difference is that Muslims call their quest "the *shari'a*."[36]

Muslims and Methodists: Building Bridges on Campus

Those of us who seek to serve faithfully as United Methodist chaplains or campus ministers in the midst of these complexities might feel deeply

---

35 See http://www.umc.org/news-and-media/same-sex-marriage-ruling-adds-to-church-debate. For an even deeper and broader review of such conflictual issues, see http://www.pewforum.org/2013/04/08/applying-gods-law-religious-courts-and-mediation-in-the-us/. For yet another perspective on Methodism in relation to the Supreme Court and the US Constitution, see https://johnmeunier.wordpress.com/2013/06/29/adam-hamilton-reax-to-supreme-court/.

36 Kadri, *Heaven on Earth*.

challenged by the issues presented here. Yet it is exactly in the midst of these complex challenges that we can claim a sense of hope for the opportunities made possible in the knowledge that Muslims and Methodists hold so much in common.

In reviewing my calling as a United Methodist pastor in ministries of higher education, now four decades-plus with memories, what I know most is that I have so much yet to learn. Even so, I am growing "comfortable in my uncomfortableness," because I now know I am not alone on this journey. What I have discovered, most importantly, is that, in the Wesleyan tradition of higher education in The United Methodist Church, we possess a particularly rich cache of resources to address these concerns.

> Rather than either isolating faith as something outside the curriculum or mandating a particular set of beliefs, United Methodist-related colleges and universities provide courses and co-curricular programs that enable students to delve into questions of meaning and purpose. Support for students by faculty, administrators, peers, and even United Methodists in the community is an important part of the blend of excellence in academics, commitment to community, and integration of faith with learning that is decidedly United Methodist.[37]

Within this shared vision of ministry in higher education, I am buoyed all the more by this specific United Methodist commitment to our efforts in Christian-Muslim ventures:

> The intent in developing interreligious relationships is not to amalgamate all faiths into one religion. We Christians have no interest in such syncretism. To engage in interreligious dialogue is neither to endorse nor to deny the faith of other people. In dialogue we mutually seek insight into the wisdom of other traditions and we hope to overcome our fears and misapprehensions. Far from requiring a lessening of commitment to Christ, effective dialogue is only possible when one's own faith is strong, and may ultimately serve to deepen or extend it.

---

37 *Handbook for Leaders of United Methodist-Related Schools, Colleges, and Universities* (Nashville: General Board of Higher Education and Ministry, 2015), 3. See http://www.gbhem.org/sites/default /files/documents/education/UM_Leaders_Handbook2015.pdf.

We Christians are seeking to be neighbors with persons whose religious commitments are different from our own and to engage each other about the deepest convictions of our lives. In our assurance of and trust in God's grace in Jesus Christ, we open ourselves to dialogue and engagement with persons of other faith communities and to other Christians whose understandings, cultures, and practices may be different from our own.

This interreligious engagement challenges United Methodist Christians to think in new ways about our lives in the broader human community, about our mission, evangelism, service, and our life together within the Christian church. We seek to promote peace and harmony with persons of other religious traditions in our various towns, cities, and neighborhoods. Yet we do not hide our differences, nor avoid conflicts, but seek to make them constructive. In each place, we share our lives with each other, we witness and are witnessed to, we invite others into the Christian community and we are invited into theirs. Our prayer is that the lives of all in each place will be enriched by the differences of others, that a new sense of community may emerge, and that others may receive the gift of God in Christ, while we receive the gifts which have been given them.[38]

There are so many ways for each of us to live out this call to a broader and deeper campus ministry, with Methodists and Muslims living better together in our midst.

I pray it may be so.

Select Bibliography

Esposito, John. *What Everyone Needs to Know About Islam*. Oxford: Oxford University Press, 2002.

Patel, Eboo. *InterFaith Leadership: A Primer*. Boston: Beacon Press, 2016.

Patel, Eboo. *Sacred Ground: Pluralism, Prejudice, and the Promise of America*. Boston: Beacon Press, 2012.

Patel, Eboo, and Patrice Brodeur, eds. *Building the Interfaith Youth Movement: Beyond Dialogue to Action*. Lanthan: Rowman & Littlefield Publishers, 2006.

---

38 *Handbook*, 5, citing *The United Methodist Book of Resolutions*, Ecumenical Issues, 3141, "Called to Be Neighbors and Witnesses: Guidelines for Interreligious Relationships, Intent."

BREAKING BREAD, BUILDING RELATIONSHIPS

Living the Sacrament to Create the Beloved Community

Jeanne Roe Smith

Campus Minister, Wesley Foundation Serving UCLA, 580 Café

ass shootings. Sexual assault. Racial inequity. Income inequality. Homelessness. Educational access. Deportation. Mass incarceration. Extrajudicial killings. Homophobia. Islamophobia. Religious bigotry. Emotional and physical abuse. Gender persecution. Political instability. Environmental destruction. Every day in the news, in social media, in our interactions with others, we experience the fragmentation and fear that shapes our daily lives. On our campuses we are all too familiar with the realities that come along with these. Students, faculty, and staff participate in "crisis response" training for active shooter scenarios, gender and sexuality awareness, disaster preparedness. Students come to university with hope and expectation to

This chapter is a culmination of conversations, stories, and insights of the community of 580 Café. Participatory engagement in developing the ethos and concepts of 580 Café is fundamental to living out our call to beloved community. It is with deep gratitude and respect to all who participate and help shape community at 580 that this chapter is offered to build and become the beloved community together.

169

achieve their educational and professional goals yet are often unprepared for the personal and emotional struggles they encounter. Along with demanding academic programs, students must learn to navigate the social, emotional, and spiritual highways that influence their time at university. While this is a daunting task for many, it is especially difficult for students who already face displacement based on ethnicity, race, orientation, economics, mental and physical capacity, gender, gender identity, or sexuality.

The theological imperative of collegiate ministry is to engage college students' faith, reason, experience, and practice to develop principled leaders both locally and globally. How then does the faith community empower, educate, and invite students who already are at the margins of the academic community into a life of hope, grace, and justice? What is the role, if any, of the faith community in addressing these issues? Can the faith community provide insight and action (praxis) to create a more just and accessible educational system, especially in higher education? Will the faith community build relationships not only with students but with faculty, staff, and administration to address the overarching issues, system dysfunction, and marginalization, to provide excellence in education for all?

This chapter will explore how the relationship of faith and reason builds the bridge to inclusion and access. It will describe how Wesley Foundation Serving University of California, Los Angeles, addresses the challenge of living faithfully with students displaced and marginalized by systems of racism, classism, homophobia, nationalism, and ideology. The 580 Café as the model for intentional action to identify and address the systems that dehumanize and diminish displaced students' sacred worth provides the framework to create a community of grace and compassion with, for, and by those most displaced by systemic oppression.

Theological Framework

The Christian community is called to emulate and incarnate life in Christ; to live in ways that make Christ known in word, action, and attitude. To engage with the world and campus, we first must find ways to welcome all whom we encounter, not only those known to us or who are like us. "Welcome one another, therefore, just as Christ has welcomed you, for the glory of God" (Romans 15:7) establishes the premise for how we are to welcome others in our daily living. It is not enough to only welcome; we must acknowledge the goodness and sacred worth of all creation. Again, scripture reminds us "For everything created by God is good, and nothing is to be rejected, provided it is received with thanksgiving; for it is sanctified by God's word and by prayer" (1 Timothy 4:4-5). Recognition of the sacred worth of others, and of the grace of God to welcome all, then calls us to include and honor all people. "For by grace you have been saved through faith, and this is not your own doing; it is the gift of God—not the result of works, so that no one may boast. For we are what he has made us, created in Christ Jesus for good works" (Ephesians 2:8-10).

We embody these scriptures when we participate in Holy Communion—remembering the welcome of God to the table of grace, the blessing of the meal of Jesus—who was broken, shared, and sent into the world to make God's love, justice, and grace known to all. Holy Communion is more than a ritual to remember and nourish believers' souls; it becomes a practical way to live life in communion with all creation. Communion becomes the practice of acknowledging the blessing, brokenness, and sharing of life together as we move in a world that is at odds with hope, healing, and compassion. When we embrace Communion as a radical act of transformation and resistance to the negative powers of displacement, we begin to heal the world with God's love and justice. We are able to recognize the image of God within those who have not been included in the usual structures and systems. We become whole and holy when we seek to create and practice communion-ity with those whom society has displaced and cast aside. The spiritual discipline of emerging scriptural understanding, engaging social concerns, and faithful response drive collegiate ministry.

The Role of the Faith Community in Higher Education

"Each of us must please our neighbor for the good purpose of building up the neighbor. For whatever was written in former days was written for our instruction, so that by steadfastness and by the encouragement of the scriptures we might have hope" (Romans 15:2, 4).

In the twenty-first century The United Methodist Church has a unique opportunity to engage this centuries-old challenge in powerful and faithful ways. The recognition of the need for presence, praxis, and prayer for university students is deeply rooted in our Wesleyan heritage. The Methodist movement began on the campus of Oxford University with John and Charles Wesley and their "Holy Club" of college students, concerned with and called to living their faith and belief in real and authentic ways. Their work was based on their emerging understanding of Holy Scripture, the social concerns they faced, and the faithful response they were compelled to create.

Hospitality is a primary focus of collegiate ministry, welcoming students to university and providing a space to explore the deep questions of life, work, and community. More than just a continuation of faith formation for Methodist students, collegiate ministry is a place for students who are curious about faith, belief, and God to learn, grow, and experience faith in ways that engage their heart, mind, and soul. Engaging with new ideas, information, and people helps to develop the moral, ethical, and professional capacity of students as they continue to expand and deepen their beliefs and practices along with their academic studies. Taken together, these prepare students for the challenges ahead, creating a strong foundation of knowledge, faith, and experience.

Hospitality is more than just being nice or greeting new people politely. It is more than offering college students food and fun activities. When understood as a spiritual practice, it becomes an avenue to engage with others where they are and as they are, with respect for and recognition of their inherent sacred worth. This type of hospitality calls us to deepen our understanding of welcome and connection beyond a handshake and introduction at the door. Hospitality illuminates our moral compass, guiding us into new directions, relationships, and possibilities by taking us out of our comfort zones and into the world around.

Rev. Dr. Marilyn Sewell reminds us that, as we extend our hospitality beyond our own doors and practices, "We are a church, and it is appropriate that we ask ourselves, what is the moral dimension of our hospitality, the moral dimension of our reception of others, of our solidarity with others, who may not look like us or move from the same assumptions or values?"[1] The practice of radical hospitality offers the expansive welcome of God in ways that are authentic and life-giving. "Offer them Christ," the words of commissioning to Thomas Coke by John Wesley as he left for the British colonies, still hold true today as we embark in ministry with college students. Moving beyond handing out tracts on campus and event-driven worship, offering Christ in real and tangible ways connects students to a God who is more than entertainment and morality rules. It is offering students CHRIST, Compassion, Hope, Relationship, Inspiration, Sanctuary, and Truth, in ways that spark their imagination, engage their spirit, and nourish their soul. It mirrors the communion call to bless, share, and serve others with life-giving opportunities to address brokenness and fear. In honoring the blessing and brokenness of self and others, offering CHRIST reminds us of what Christ invites all to experience, share, and receive.

John Wesley's call to practice our faith in Christ in community is an important guideline for ministry: "The Gospel of Christ knows no religion but social, no holiness but social."[2] His deep concern for the poor and those disenfranchised by systems of power and access remains relevant in our discourse on ministry with displaced persons. This radical notion that all are welcome at God's table is evidenced in the United Methodist invitation for Communion. Rather than needing to be a member of a certain congregation or denomination, United Methodist Communion is open to "all who believe or earnestly seek to believe in Christ Jesus." In making this statement, we assert Communion is not simply a rite of passage or belonging but an act of invitation and inclusion; an opening to the heart of God for all, no exceptions,

---

1   Rev. Dr. Marilyn Sewell, "Radical Hospitality," Unitarian Universalist Association, Jan. 21, 2015, accessed Apr. 17, 2018, https://www.uua.org/worship/words/sermon/radical-hospitality.

2   Kevin M. Watson, Vital Piety Blog, "Prooftexting Wesley," Mar. 12, 2010, https://vitalpiety.com/2010/03/12/prooftexting-wesley/.

no limits, just the sincere and earnest desire to live in Christ and as Christ for all the world to see. It is an act of grace and mercy not controlled by human restrictions; an act of the Holy Spirit, mandated by God and incarnated by Christ Jesus. When we use this model for engaging with students displaced by violence, orientation, ethnicity, gender, culture, we must first recognize their inherent blessing—created in the image of God, and blessed as a part of the people of God.

This initial recognition of blessing provides a positive and affirming way of identifying self and others as valued and valuable. This is the individual's way of claiming our identity (name) and how that identity is expressed in relationship to how we see ourselves and others in the world. We name our unique characteristics and value and ultimately our imago Dei when we are able to see God's blessing and love in our self and identity in Christ. Engaging students in this process of actively affirming theirs and other's imago Dei offers them the ability to recognize their value and worth even as they experience displacement, suffering, and trauma. This act of honoring and affirming students first as blessed and beloved creations of a loving God is often in stark contrast with the labels and systems society imposes upon them.

Labels are identifiers that organize and situate people into categories that can be both positive and negative to self-worth. When labels affirm and uplift people, they are useful in naming and claiming healthy relationship. Choosing those labels that affirm and demonstrate our "name" and sacred worth empowers and reminds us of our connection to each other and God. Labels, though, can also be mechanisms of displacement, used to diminish the value of a person or persons and add to the challenge of seeing value or worth in self, family, others. When these labels exclude, shame, or deny our sacred worth, dignity, and humanity, we must provide ways to reframe, change, or detach these labels and assumptions to stay connected to our name and relationships in ways that are life-giving and transformative.

By helping students identify the labels that separate them from their sacred worth, we equip them with the ability to embrace their capacity and dignity in the midst of societal constructs and systems that seek to deny their rightful place at God's table. To claim one's name and place in God's community becomes an act of acceptance and affirmation as well as an act of resistance to the systems of the world that seek to deny and displace us. When we share our stories, hopes, dreams, and struggles, we again discover the mystery of God revealed. In this relationship of sacred blessing, brokenness, and sharing we encounter the living God among and between us. We remember the power and compassion of Christ who draws all to seek justice, love kindness, and walk humbly with God and each other.

We must first examine our own understandings and assumptions about grace, compassion, and sacred worth. We must move beyond an elementary understanding of God's hope and promise, which is purely personal and self-centered, into a deeper, more expansive wisdom that guides and directs our uneasy steps of faith and practice. We must challenge and examine critically the doctrinal and creedal statements that do not uphold or affirm the expansiveness of God's inclusive and radical love if we are to be faithful to God's communion call—that grace and love is available without exception for all.

Campus ministry, by its unique location and relationship to higher education, provides not only The United Methodist Church but other faith communities the opportunity to engage in scholarly inquiry and critical thinking about how to live more fully and faithfully into our communion call. The blessing of involvement with students engaged in academic studies, especially those that relate to political, social, health, and personal well-being, requires the church to grow in faith, wisdom, and understanding. Sharing blessing and brokenness in study, history, and personal experience builds understanding between different cultures and traditions viewed through the lens of common humanity and dignity. Once blessing and brokenness are recognized, sharing the common cup and bread of education opens our eyes and hearts to see the fullness and expanse of creation. No longer can we deny the integrity, value, or humanity of another. No longer can we sit idly by while others perish from hunger, disease, and poverty. No longer can we claim our place at the table when others are denied because of their race, gender, nationality, sexuality, or economic status. Once we have embraced Communion as a *sacramental act of daily living*, we must find ways to live out our commitment to go into the world and be living examples of Christ's life-giving love.

The Relationship of the Faith Community to Create Systemic Change

A long legacy of social justice activism is at the core of Wesley Foundation Serving UCLA's ministry. Offering support and advocacy for Japanese American citizens post–World War II, engaging women in leadership in the 1950s, providing counsel for Conscientious Objectors in the 1960s, and becoming the first Reconciling in Christ campus ministry in the early 1990s, Wesley Foundation Serving UCLA has been at the forefront of justice-making at the university and in the community, engaging students, campus, and congregations in addressing social injustice and challenging systems of oppression through action, education, and theological reflection. Faith informed by scripture, reason, experience, and tradition is a tenet of Wesleyan theology that is utilized in engaging students, faculty, staff, and community in vital relationships in our work to create God's beloved community. We are guided by our understanding of scripture and its application to our life together on campus and in the world.

In April 2009, Wesley Foundation was invited into a dialogue with the Vice Chancellor of Student Affairs office to address issues of hunger and housing insecurity on campus. In the discussions that followed, concern was raised for students facing economic and financial challenges in accessing food and housing. Specific populations of students identified by Student Affairs officials were undocumented students, first-generation college students, former foster youth, and students identifying as LGBTQ. The initial discussion focused on ways that Wesley Foundation Serving UCLA could provide food resources to these groups. What began as a simple request to provide food for hungry students would grow into the 580 Café.

The Wesley Foundation Serving UCLA staff, recognizing the invitation to develop community with students experiencing marginalization because of economic factors as a call to justice, designed the 580 Café as a space for students to not only find food but develop a community of respect and care. Fundamental to this process is the recognition that students, no matter their socioeconomic status, race, creed, family configuration, or orientation, are all created in the image of God, and as such are blessed and valuable *as they are*. Whatever their backstory, students are first and foremost beloved and blessed by the God of all creation and are only displaced because of societal, cultural, and political systems. There is no such thing as a displaced child of God, only someone marginalized by systems and structures that are designed to keep them out or deny their inherent dignity and capacity. A guiding principle of Methodism is that no one is beyond the reach of God's love, and we are called to help others experience that love in ways the build up and affirm each other.

Sharing hopes, dreams, joys, sorrows, and concerns daily, not only as the sacramental ritual of Communion but as a daily expression of God's grace, presence, and movement in the lives of students, is a primary function of the 580 Café. Drawing together all those who seek nourishment both physically and spiritually in a space that affirms one's dignity and sacred worth becomes a practical application of living sacramentally in community.

Recognizing the sacred worth (blessing) that each student brings is the first part of living out our communion call at the 580 Café. No one is denied access or entrance—all are welcome to participate and share in community. The one requirement of all who participate is to respect the dignity and value of self and others who are part of the community. While this is a simple concept, it can be a tall order given the current reality that many students face. Respect and civil conduct sets the standard for students' interactions, especially when they encounter ideas, cultures, traditions, and practices vastly different from their own. This is consistent with acknowledging not only the blessing but the brokenness of each, and developing compassionate responses and understandings to establish respect and kindness for all.

It is not enough to recognize blessing; it is imperative to acknowledge and address as well the brokenness that brings students to the 580 Café. The Social Principles of The United Methodist Church provide a framework for engagement with systems and people impacted by violence, migration, racism, sexism, and economic justice. Being open to discuss the root causes of racism, sexism, homophobia, and religious intolerance in an honest and thoughtful way encourages students to enter into deeper dialogue and explore personal biases, religious teachings, and societal systems that deny the sacred worth of others and themselves. In opening the dialogue on brokenness, students then are able to share the causes of their displacement in a context of respect and compassion and recognize their own sacred worth, independent of structural violence and systemic oppression. In learning that there are actual social principles that undergird The United Methodist Church and its work to create a more just and caring world, students unfamiliar or distanced from the gospel of Christ begin to see a way of being "The Church" that is not coercive, oppressive, or manipulative but is governed by actions guided by faith and informed by scripture and reason. It is indeed a radical notion that an institution that operates in the system of authority and power over others also works to create equality, peace, and inclusion.

Understanding these cultural, religious, and societal barriers and intentionally opening dialogue about these made coming to the 580 Café less intimidating. Students, while at first leery of "church" or Christians offering free food and study space, began to see the 580 Café as a place to ask difficult questions, challenge conventional thinking, and explore ways to understand others from different backgrounds and beliefs.

The "sharing" element of Communion takes place around tables, on couches, and during lively discussions of world events, academic research, and day-to-day life as a young adult. By sharing their truth, experience, and insights, students participate in communal healing and hope—even during times of disagreement and dissension. Students then are sent back onto campus or to work or home enriched by their time together; engaged in sharing new ideas, hopes, and dreams; feeling affirmed and respected and able to take on the tasks or challenges of the day ahead with renewed minds and spirits. The 580 Café is an intentional space for students to participate in a community that recognizes them as valuable and valued members, now—accepting them as they are, regardless of where they are from and who they are becoming.

The Role of the 580 Café in the Lives of Students Displaced by Systems of Oppression

Open since February 2010 after time spent in discussion with students, campus officials, and community members with the goal of listening to the needs and concerns expressed by displaced students, the 580 Café offers hot meals and study space for any student brave enough to cross the street and leave campus behind. The 580 Café is situated in St. Alban's Episcopal Church, at a main entrance to UCLA and at a primary bus stop. The space for the 580 Café was chosen because it represents both an ancient and contemporary connection to faith and a convenient location near campus. The 580, as students refer to it, is a room located in the center of the church complex just off the front patio, where students find a homelike atmosphere. When they enter the 580 students find a large refrigerator, couch, and two large tables that provide seating and eating space. There is a counter with a microwave, coffee maker, and toaster oven to prepare food. There are cupboards full of food items to select and shelves with eating utensils, plates, cups, and napkins. Students are free to select whatever items they wish to prepare. There is no charge for the food, thanks to the generosity of alumni, congregations, families, and local businesses. The room celebrates the diverse student community with student artwork, a bulletin board with pictures of students as children, and posters that celebrate the diversity of all. There is intentional placement of church-related icons including a cross, a rainbow stole, and posters reflecting the social justice positions of The United Methodist Church to make visible our commitment to justice and inclusion. Students new to the space are often inquisitive about what it means to be a reconciling community and an immigrant-welcoming community. These are always met with a discussion of our belief in the sacred worth of all God's people and our belief that all families are sacred.

Since opening in 2010, the 580 Café has grown in participation and ministry with, by, and of students. Open daily 8 a.m. to 6 p.m., the 580 Café operates as a student-run space. Student coordinators make sure the café is open on time, supplies are put out fresh each day, the space is left clean and tidy each evening, and anyone who enters is welcomed with a smile and a brief orientation to how the space works. Students are encouraged to care for the upkeep and atmosphere of the café and are incredibly clear on keeping it a safe and friendly place for students.

Students who have experienced displacement are central to how the 580 Café operates. They are integral to the leadership, handling the food and up-keep of the café as well as defining, creating, and fostering community. For example, the Art and Soul group was initiated by an undocumented student who wanted to create a space for art, activism, and healing. Providing cre-ative ways to express their frustrations, fears, and hopes became a conduit to healing, as students were able to express themselves artistically and engage others in reflection and discussion on such an expression. As one leader in the Art and Soul group graduated, another student stepped up to offer her experience and faith by leading. Renamed Heart Lab, the group took a more focused look at scripture, art, and expression, continuing to provide a heal-ing, hopeful space for students to explore their faith and beliefs together.

To gather students together to think theologically about their shared experience from a lens of Christian scripture and practice, Open Table of-fers students fellowship, a common meal, scripture reflection, and prayer to deepen their faith and understanding of God. Held mid-week, at Open Table students find a place to unpack the stress and worry of the week by engaging in active discussion and reflection on scripture and practice. Open Table invites all students who come to 580 Café to share what it means to be a Christian, even those who are of other faith traditions, no tradition, or skeptical. No pressure or judgement is made on students who do not claim Christian faith; rather they are invited to participate and learn more about spiritual practices, ideas, and wisdom. Many have remarked that they enjoy being able to think differently about how they live and what their beliefs are, and they have asked to attend Sunday worship at local churches with the worship group. Open Table creates a time and space for students to unplug and recharge, to think about their lives in ways that they often avoid or otherwise do not have time for. In the chaotic lives they lead, and for some, the displacement they endure, the café is a healing space that restores their souls and reminds them of their inherent worth and dignity.

By sharing the foundations of faith, through fellowship, food, and worship, students engage with others in dispelling the bonds of displacement, disenfranchisement, and separation from each other, their families, their communities, and God. When they are able to challenge the systems that have displaced them and find a space where they are loved and affirmed they find within themselves and others the image of God and the community of God made visible in their midst. Their daily lives are not simply something to be endured but instead full of promise and life and possibilities, because in this space, they recognize and claim their sacred worth and begin to share that with others. "For, in fact, the kingdom of God is among [us]" (Luke 17:21).

How do students describe their experience at the 580 Café? For some it is the place they can come, meet with friends, and have some free food. For others it is a place to study and take a break from their rigorous academic and work routines. And others find it a place where they can bring their sorrow and wounds and find care and compassion. At the 580 Café, those displaced by society find they are able to be their true selves, without labels or stigma. One student put it this way: "When I come to the 580 I can take off the labels the university and world have put on me, and here I can just be me; what a relief that is!" Another student offered that the 580 is a place for students to find solidarity with others in their experience of the challenges at the university and within the community. What better way to engage with students displaced by systems of exclusion and oppression than to offer them CHRIST in ways that affirm their worth, ignite their imaginations, and encourage their paths to wholeness and holiness? Living and loving sacramentally with students, especially those whom society marginalizes and discards, is possible when together we create spaces that value and uplift the dignity and capacity of each.

The value of such spaces for college students and the greater campus community becomes obvious in times of crisis and trauma. In a year fraught with interpersonal violence and death on campus, the 580 Café has been a place for students to gather to share their fears and worries and find comfort together. Recently, a campus shooting put the entire campus on lockdown for over four hours. The 580 provided shelter and sanctuary to over twenty students, faculty, and staff. Students who had not heard of the urgent need to stay off campus were met at the bus stop and encouraged to seek shelter at the 580 until the situation was under control. Staff being told to exit the building where the shooting was taking place initially had nowhere to go. They too found security and a space to wait at the 580 Café. Some had come because they knew a church was on that corner (where the 580 Café is located); others simply were trying to find a place to seek shelter. As the events unfolded, much prayer and concern was shared by the group. Many of the regular 580 Café students texted and called to check in on the space and those who were there. Once the situation was under control students poured in to the café to share their worries and fears. The 580 became a hub of healing and hugs—inviting those who needed comfort and people to be with.

In the days that followed, the 580 offered space to student groups, faculty, and staff to come together and heal. Because the 580 Café is set up as a safe zone for all, the infrastructure to respond to crisis on campus or in the world, we were able to be immediately present and available to any and all who sought sanctuary. Our daily presence of welcoming all, and respecting all, provides the much-needed framework to be a vital and healing presence every day—during times of crisis as well as the day-to-day struggle to become whole and productive. For those who daily experience the microaggressions of race, gender, sexuality, immigration, and ability, the 580 Café is their safe space to remember their value and dignity. This is the mission of the church, to offer CHRIST to all and to be present in the process of transforming the world into God's Beloved Community.

Conclusion and Final Reflections

We must learn to love first—to eliminate labels that separate us and limit the fullness of God. The student community at the 580 Café has humbled and inspired our journey with college students. Rather than assuming they need to be taught and managed, we should realize students offer new insights and opportunities to what it means to live fully, faithfully, and joyfully, even when circumstances would seem contradictory. The 580 Café community is a vibrant place where all dwell free—free to be who they are—without shame, excuse, or exception. Our students come from God's rich tapestry of culture, belief, language, and traditions. And yet, the thread that weaves us and binds us together in common concern is that love knows no borders, colors, doctrine, or capacity. While the campus, church, and world may yet be unable to cross those borders, students who are living with the impact of displacement and exclusion are creating new pathways to peace and justice by learning to live and love together in spaces like the 580 Café, where they learn to "celebrate life, engage God, and love all."

The 580 Café is a gift offered not only to the students who are served and share communion-ity within it but also for The United Methodist Church, and the privilege and power it holds. The gift to both is best expressed by a former student who still comes by the 580 to connect with the spirit of kindness and love she finds there. "The 580 is a place where I found family [and] friends and for the first time in my life was welcomed by an institution of power and privilege and treated with kindness, respect, and love." If we are to become the Beloved Community, then we must find ways to dismantle the systems of exclusion that make others feel unwelcome and unwanted.

To create and sustain a community like the 580 Café we must first examine our own privilege and assumptions. We must learn to live the gospel call to love God and love neighbor as we are loved. We must work together— alongside and in solidarity with those who have been displaced by colonialism, nationalism, racism, homophobia, heteropatriarchy, and anything that denies the sacred worth and dignity of all people. For those of us who represent the dominant culture, tradition, and power, we must acknowledge our complicity in the displacement of God's own beloved children and seek forgiveness from those we have excluded, and repent of our actions that continue to displace and oppress the Beloved Community.

We must demand that our institutions of higher education and church authority acknowledge the systemic oppression of cultures, communities, and peoples and develop new pathways to peace and justice. Education offers us the opportunity to enter into real dialogue and praxis as we work together to live sacramentally—to become more fully aware and active in global governance. As United Methodists we are called to participate in the healing of the world so that all may know Christ, recognizing the world is our parish, not our plaything. We must tend the souls and spirits of those in our midst with the love, respect, and justice that God offers us. To do anything less would deny Christ and leave the world wanting and waiting for a savior to truly believe in. It is time for Church to be the living loving presence of Christ—to put an end to displacing people, cultures, and families; to embrace and work toward building and becoming God's Beloved Community here and now.

FORCED MIGRATION AND ITS IMPACT ON NEW MODELS OF FAMILY LIFE

Daniel Alberto Trujillo

Latin American Theology Professor, United
Methodist Church in Honduras

Introduction

The realities of displacement, or forced migration, and the economic situation that we are presently experiencing in Central America have a significant impact on the configuration of new models of family life, affecting emotional bonding and forms of family interaction in different ways.

I justify this approach from my experience as an immigrant and my work in providing psychological and pastoral care to families who have suffered the departure of a father or a mother who has gone to other countries (for instance, the United States and Spain) in search of a better future for the immigrant and his or her family.

From these work experiences and bibliographical research, two points are raised: first, a descriptive and critical analysis is made of the new psychosocial and economic realities arising from forced migration to other countries by either the father or the mother for the purpose of presenting the models of family life that are developed according to the impact of forced migration.

Next, through biblical and theological analysis, the issue of immigrant rights in the Bible is addressed as a reality that has always existed, and from that reality how to influence policies and advocate on behalf of immigrant rights today is determined.

Psychosocial and Economic Analysis within the Central American Context in Which the Causes That Foment Forced Migration Are Presented

In the last two decades, Central America has experienced the growing reality of forced migration, and, failing that, mass deportations. This is why many Central Americans leave their countries of origin, no longer in search of the American dream but rather to flee the nightmare of life in their violent communities. People flee in search of shelter or work, or simply to seek a better life, since their societies are afflicted by pain and suffering produced by organized crime, including drug trafficking, money laundering, *maras* [gangs], extortion, sexual exploitation, and sex trafficking, among others coupled with government corruption and existing weak institutions. In this forced exile of Central American immigrants to the United States, few are able to successfully complete their journey.

The extreme security measures of the Mexican and US governments regarding the containment of the flow of Central American immigrants migrating north violate the most fundamental human rights—respect for life and freedom of movement. Male and female immigrants who are caught for being undocumented are profiled, often considered delinquents, terrorists, or gang members. Added to this reality are the many humiliations suffered on the immigrant's journey, where he or she encounters terrible ordeals such as assault, rape, incarceration, and death by starvation in the desert or at the hands of the *Zetas*, an armed group working for Mexican drug cartels (for example, ninety-eight Honduran immigrants were massacred at San Fernando ranch in Tamaulipas, Mexico, in 2010). Even after living through such traumatic experiences and being deported, they attempt to cross the Rio Grande again, since life expectancy in Central America, due to overwhelming economic problems, becomes less favorable with each day that passes. From this perspective, external forced migration is a concrete reality in the region, rooted socially and economically in such a way that it is repeated over and over, in spite of its consequences.

When speaking of forced migration abroad, we are not talking about someone who wants to travel but someone who at a certain point has no other choice but to potentially migrate toward death. The choice is between dying lying down without hope or dying standing up. Persons who migrate choose the latter, exercising the right to reject a silent and resigned death as opposed to a system that restricts and annihilates every option for life. Hope, therefore, is built upon risk (Brisson 1997, 13).

The region of Central America is experiencing a reality that is full of despair, including unimaginable rates of unemployment, extreme violence, and political corruption. Faced with this situation of oppression and suffering, there is no other option than to emigrate by force. The region does not offer any guarantee of a better future; the current economic model has promoted increased taxes, the privatization of the majority of state-owned enterprises, growing inflation in the cost of basic necessities, and the increased cost of public services. Above all, growing public fear and insecurity produced by organized crime forces many Central Americans to leave; migration in this sense is seen as one of the few possibilities of getting ahead. The other option is to participate in *narco menudeo* [selling drugs in the streets] or organized crime, in order to be able to survive. But between these two options the majority chooses to migrate.

> Migration becomes an opportunity, a way out. Immigration is not a choice; it is a last resource, and it is widely known that if so many people flee, it is because within it all lies a desert of hunger and desperation. Formerly, people migrated with the promise of improvement; now they migrate with a good deal of despair. They do not know whether their lot is going to be better; what they do know is that they cannot stay where they are. (Brisson 1997, 113)

In this sense, it is important to emphasize that the phenomenon of forced external migration and its social, economic, and emotional implications are part of, or a consequence of, the exclusionary capitalist system that dom-inates third world societies, given that migration itself is an underground resource for this capitalist system, as well as other social problems such as criminality, disintegration of families, and drug trafficking.

From this perspective, forced migration carries terrible consequences at a psychosocial level for the people who leave as well as the ones who stay behind, and it has an immediate impact on the family, especially on women and their children.

> Immigration has a considerable impact on those who remain in their place of origin, which includes the dismantling of various families due to the fact that when the father leaves, he finds new conditions of life that lead him to reorganize his life in the receiving country, forgetting his original family. It is then that the woman has to take on the entire economic responsibility as well as the education of the children. (Brisson 1997, 115)

In this migratory process, the family is most affected at a physical, eco-nomic, and, above all, emotional level; the family becomes fragmented when one of its members, in this case the father, leaves the home. In reading M. R. Radillo regarding migratory processes and their impact on the family, we can see some of these consequences.

> The migration process brings serious complications within the family's life. It is not possible to ignore its implications when working with immigrants. Every migratory process produces total or partial disloca-tion of the person. It represents the loss of significant aspects of life and the risk of serious complications and emotional traumas, which may affect persons for years and, we may add, their families. (Radillo 2011, 145)

Migrating is a traumatic process, as much for the person who migrates as for the family that remains. Often one does not migrate because one wishes to, as we mentioned previously; it is done because the state of insecurity and the economic and social situation of the migrant is dismal, without options for a better future, especially when the migrant has family responsibilities that involve raising and educating children.

But in spite of this panorama, after the migrant achieves the goal of arriving at the receiving country, other realities present themselves that directly affect the family; the family breaks up and loses its configuration, and new models of family life arise: transnational families, blended families, families that have their own psychosocial realities.

Transnational Families, Reunification, Adaptation, and Encounter with the Family

Before reflecting on a new model of family life, the definition of the term "transnationalism" will be addressed:

> Transnationalism, applied to the phenomenon of migration, is based on the fact that migrants maintain multiple family, economic, social, organizational, religious and political relations which overcome borders. They carry out actions, make decisions and develop identities within social networks that keep them connected with two or more societies simultaneously. (Basch, Glick Schiller, and Blanc-Szanton 1992, 12)

As a mode of analysis, families are not exempt from the phenomenon of migration as to new configurations of models of family life; in this case, these models are the so-called transnational families. From this perspective, we define this model of a family in the following way: it involves those families in which some of the members are in the country of origin and others in the destination country. "The reuniting of its members creates a tension that maintains the family as a unit beyond distance" (Sánchez 2004, 32).

In the ideal of the legal documented migrant who leaves his family in the country of origin, the migrant does not lose the hope of an early encounter or reencounter, or reunification, as Sánchez mentions. But the current reality of the other, the illegal immigrant, is different; their legal status does not allow them even to dream about bringing their families, since by the very condition of illegality, they themselves endure the latent danger of being deported. Here, reunion will only occur after the immigrant is able to pay all the debts left behind, save a considerable amount of money to return to the country of origin, and start a business in order to survive, improve their quality of life, and move forward.

In this sense, in order to achieve the reunification of the family, immigrants will need to work every day, twelve to fourteen hours a day, and live in a crowded apartment with seven other persons in order to lower the cost of rent and bills. Above all, they will have to persevere until they fulfill their ultimate objectives, besides sending money at the end of every month so that the family left behind can survive. This purpose can take them three or five years, depending on work conditions, which today are scarce and uncertain. This is the case of immigrants who do not want to lose connection with their families, since the idea of reunification encourages them to work hard in the hope of a prompt reencounter. But this does not mean that the immigrant and his family of origin and the family, friends, or community of fellow nationals who receive him do not maintain economic and social relations with him, since social networks exist that have been opened and strengthened with the passing of time, creating communities and entire transnational neighborhoods where the reunification or reencounter can take place once legal status is reached.

> But reunification is not the only element that defines the transnational family; there is also the element of survival. Normally, he or the members that are in the destination country, through the means provided by technology, not only maintain communication with the family members in the society of origin, but they contribute economically to its survival, generally through the money sent and the purchase of properties. (Sánchez 2004, 33)

Upholding the ideal of reencounter or reunification, the entire family is involved in spite of psychosocial problems such as low self-esteem, dropping out of school, aggressive and antisocial behavior, abandonment, insecurity, fear, drug addiction, and street life, which arise because of the absence of the father or mother. The family seeks the healthiest ways of restructuring roles and rules for its adaptive functioning. "The task of adaptation is, for many persons, arduous and complicated; perceived even as unattainable. The task becomes more difficult because it is necessary to add the role that immigration plays in exacerbating family conflicts as these same conflicts are addressed" (Radillo 2011, 146).

> Therefore, the restructuring of the family reaches deep levels, which make a post-immigration renegotiation necessary. The roles of gender, as well as family values, usually differ in the new medium as well as the place of origin, which implies an inevitable effect on the relationship between spouses and generations. (Vuornien 2003, 21)

The adaptation makes evident that the family is not a closed unit that remains unaltered in the face of new environments that modify its dynamics. Stability and change become great challenges to family development; "the family can be considered as a system in constant transformation, which means that it is capable of adapting to the demands of individual development of its members and to the demands of its surroundings; this adaptation ensures the continuity and, at the same time, the psychosocial growth of the members" (Lila 2000).

From this perspective, the transnational family as a new model of family life, which arises out of the phenomenon of forced migration, is a new reality of family life. Therefore, transnational families constitute a domestic unit in which some of its members live in another country and where there are economic ties and bonds of survival that are maintained on the basis of the tension of family reunification. They constitute a deterritorialization of the family, and this puts the traditional concept of the nuclear family model in check (Vuornien 2003, 22). Unfortunately, the transnational family is not a choice but rather the result of conditions of despair and forced migration and an attempt to better quality of life.

In this section we set forth the concept of the transnational family and the ideal of reunification as a utopian horizon to overcome obstacles, but the other face of reality also exists, one where the migrant forgets about, and marginalizes, his or her family and leaves it worse off than it was. In this sense, it is from a perspective of uprooting and marginalization that leads to a proposed description and critical analysis of the emotional, social, and economic realities found in the next section. The transnational family is left fragmented, and out of these realities new family models are formed.

Fragmented Family: Between Honor and Shame

Families fragmented by forced migration contend with honor and shame: honor through the ideal of reunification, involving the family as a unit that is conscious of its own changes, strengths, and weaknesses and fosters affective environments in spite of the absence of the paternal or maternal figure who does not break the bond; and shame, when the family is abandoned and marginalized, left on its own because the father or mother has broken the bond of affection.

The honor-reunifier (typically the wife/mother who receives money from the immigrant and saves or invests that money in buying properties in order to care for children and extended family members) acquires a status of honor within the community and the family of the husband, seeing the spouse and her children as a unit that does upholds the honor of the father who works hard in a foreign country and has suffered greatly during the journey as migrant. The community assigns symbolic honor to this mother who lives alone with her children.

From a symbolic point of view, honor represents a person's just place in society, the social position of a person. This position of honor is determined by boundaries relating to power, status based on gender, and location within the social ladder. From a functionalist point of view, honor "is the value of a person in their own eyes plus the value of said person in the eyes of their social group" (Malina 1995, 75).

But when the unfortunate happens and the husband abandons his family by forming another family abroad and leaving the original family completely marginalized in every sense, the family that stays behind, and especially the wife, suffers the shame of an unfaithful husband who abandoned her. But the most intense shame is when this woman, who has no way to support her children, ends up becoming involved with another person from the community in order to subsist or to not feel alone. "Within the woman's family, honor makes goodness or virtue implicit in her sexual exclusivity" (Malina 1995, 69). The sexual exclusivity of this abandoned woman-mother is a rule that must not be broken according to the ideal of the patriarchal ideology.

Even if the man who migrated to another country dishonors his wife by being unfaithful to her and their children, she and her children must remain in their home, bearing the humiliation.

This means that some dishonored wives turn inward, as if there were some kind of social magnet that holds them inside their homes or their cities. All the things that are carried from the inside to the outside are masculine; all the things that stay inside are feminine (Malina 1995, 69).

But faced with actual affective and economic marginalization, many women, tired of waiting, disillusioned by empty promises, leave home in search of work, to support their children. Disappointed by being abandoned, marginalized by their spouses, they end up breaking off affective relationships; although they continue to be legally married, these women start their lives over again. Shame is turned into a positive symbol. "Positive shame signifies sensitivity toward their own reputation, a sensitivity in the face of others' opinion" (Malina 1995, 70). They are no longer interested in preserving a reputation that conforms to the *machista* model, in which "the purity or sexual exclusivity of the woman is incorporated into the honor of a man" (Malina 1995, 70). On the contrary, the woman becomes dignified without a need for being in the man's shadow and she builds a reputation as a subject, where before she was in a condition of oppression and marginalization, and she is empowered as an active subject with equal rights; above all, becoming an agent as a social actor, master of her destiny and the destiny of her children. From this point of view, Malina says that

> Women who are not under the guardianship of a male (especially widows, divorcees, women without family ties) are seen as lacking feminine honor, more as men than as women, and therefore sexual predators, in a word, aggressive and dangerous. (Malina 1995, 70)

All of this produces a series of emotional problems for both the abandoned woman and her children, since they are stigmatized by the unfaithful husband's family, by the community, and even by the church or other social actors. As we mentioned previously, migration is a traumatic and ongoing event, and in cases like this even more so, since the abandoned wife and mother often has no further communication with the husband who leaves his family unprotected and subject to shame. "What is traumatic about this situation is the physical absence of the loved one, not knowing his where-abouts, the lack of real information, and not being able to say goodbye. This becomes an ambiguous loss that hinders the processing of bringing closure to a sad chapter of life" (Radillo 2011, 147). In this sense, grief be-comes complicated and the adaptive mechanisms are not sufficient to face the crisis that such ruptures bring.

In this way, a series of psychosocial problems arises: the mother has to go out and find work; in the best of cases, the children stay with their grandparents, but emotional problems still arise resulting in family violence, street life, drugs, prostitution, sexual abuse of children, or the abandonment of the children by the mother who either finds another partner or migrates, leaving them with their grandparents or aunts and uncles.

The family models within the migration phenomenon are changeable; they become configured and disconfigured according to the different dynam-ics of the family, affected as stated above by the abandonment or marginal-ization of the paternal or maternal figure. All of this connects to economic and social factors, since without money the family cannot be supported and the situations of poverty often forcibly lead to self-destructive conduct and behaviors that are hostile to human beings. But being optimistic, the abandoned woman decides to form another family; or the father who leaves forms another family abroad. From this reality, we find ourselves before a new model of family life: the blended family.

The Blended Family: New Roles, New Conflicts

The blended family is the family structure that originates in the marriage or de facto union of a couple, in which one or both of the members have children from a previous marriage or relationship. This concept of family is in terms of a "domestic group"; that is, it involves everyone who lives in the home: the new couple, the children of one or the other who come from a previous union, and the children of a new union (Grosman and Martínez Alcorta 2000, 35–36).

Faced with the phenomenon of immigration and the later abandonment of the families that are left behind, blended families take on a heightened role due to the varied conjugal ruptures on both sides of the border. Since the desire for reunification does not exist, in this case blended families arise due more to the theme of survival, although it is pertinent to point out that under this new model of family life, there are underlying different realities that often provoke conflicts among its members regarding the topic of the articulation of the family.

> This articulation between the family unit and personal development presents great obstacles to the blended family. The formation of the "we" is more difficult because the couple comes with a heavy baggage derived not only from the family of origin, but also from the previous marital bonds; life experiences, beliefs, traditions, rituals, religious conviction or educational models. The children, in turn, have experienced different patterns of behavior and disciplinary criteria that can change in the new organization. Therefore, in order for the family to acquire its own identity, and for the feeling of belonging to be generated, more time is required. (Grosman and Martínez Alcorta 58)

In view of these conflicts that arise in the articulation of these blended families, from my experience in working with immigrants what most often occurs abroad is that families that unite become rapidly separated, often because of the cultural and ideological context out of which the immigrant was born. In modern countries such as Spain or the United States, where the rights of women and children are protected, abuse and family violence are not tolerated. In this case, some Latin American men clash with laws that protect the physical and emotional integrity of women and children, and they are forced to abandon the family when they are accused of domestic violence, running the risk of being jailed or deported.

The phenomenon of immigration promotes new models of family life such as transnational families from the perspective of the illegal immigrant who holds onto the ideal of reunification of the family left behind and who works hard to gain some capital in order to improve economically. All of this fills the family with honor and gives a social status to said family within the community.

But the broken family is also reflected, the other side of reality for the illegal immigrant who leaves his family abandoned, marginalized, and in shame, where the woman must get ahead and seek survival for herself and her children. It is from these realities that other models of family life are formed, such as blended families, both abroad and within national contexts. Out of this arise psychosocial realities that affect the family. All of this is permeated by an economic reality, imposed by a dehumanizing capitalist model that provokes situations of violence and insecurity and forces people to migrate in search of better horizons; but in the long run it has a significant impact on the family, in some cases for good but in the majority of cases not.

Biblical and Theological Reflection: Theological Theory in Action

The reality of the social phenomenon of migration does not escape biblical and theological reflection, since in the Bible we find realities experienced by the people of Israel as an immigrant people and, also, concrete examples about forced migrations, such as that of Joseph, Ruth, and Jacob, among others.

In the text we also find laws that from certain perspectives or conditioning factors protect the immigrant, and an ethical and moral code concerning the duty to offer hospitality to all those who are strangers. Nowadays, in view of the problems that our immigrant brothers and sisters experience in foreign lands, with problems such as xenophobia, rejection, discrimination, violation of human rights, persecution, and every kind of arbitrary action that threatens the immigrant's very life and the survival of his or her family, it becomes necessary to approach the text looking for notable examples, and from there to reflect, with the purpose of influencing politically, so that churches abroad may join together in defense of the rights and dignity of immigrants and their families.

In the course of writing this paper, we have been studying the impact that current economic models have on our countries, and how forced immigration is a last recourse for survival, but also a problem that has direct consequences in the breakup of families and in the configuration of new models of family life.

A final point to examine is the theology of the resilient migrant, which influences readers to think in a certain way about an inclusive pastoral of the immigrant in contrast to an overwhelming capitalism where migratory movements manifest themselves as one more consequence of the unjust economic structures of humanity and of policies that generate and promote inequality among people.

From this perspective, and faced with these realities, there are duties and obligations concerning the subject that challenges us today. Christians have the responsibility of contributing to building a state ruled by the law that does not criminalize the desire to migrate, not only for those who do it out of their own free will and have sufficient resources to do it but also for those who are forced to do it, for whatever reason, as different as they may be, and even if they require assistance in solidarity. Out of the theological task, one might argue for laws that guarantee the right to migrate for all persons alike, without discrimination. This is the gratuitousness of solidarity: to guarantee the human dignity of those who, for whatever reason, expose themselves to rootlessness, asylum, loneliness, exile, displacement, refuge, or pilgrimage, whether in their own country or abroad (Duque 2004, 9).

From this theological framework found in Duque's reflection, appealing to the true reality that is implicit in the subject of migration, since migration is not the problem; the problem is the systematic violation of the immigrant's human rights when there is marked inequality and discrimination in the receiving country toward the immigrant. It is from this reality that we address immigrant rights in the Bible and how, from this theological reflection, we can influence the defense and struggle for human rights of immigrants abroad.

Theological Theory of Action

In accordance with the points that we have been developing in this article, some topics arise that seem interesting to us in order to elaborate a theoretical-theological framework of action, so that the reader may think about pastoral proposals for the work with families that are affected by rupture and crisis when they have to migrate due to the different reasons previously mentioned. In this sense, we consider the following emerging themes: exile, rootlessness, and reinsertion. From these realities we shall propose the theology of the resilient immigrant.

Exile, Rootlessness, and Reinsertion: Toward a Theology of the Resilient Immigrant

As we have discussed immigration and its consequences in the breakup of the family due to the forced departure of the family, or one of its members, some psychosocial factors arise that eventually affect the family dynamic. At this point, one might ask the following question: from where do we develop a theological reflection that helps us to understand this phenomenon? Will it be from our biblical traditions or theological heritage? Why ask this question? Because "theology remains mostly as an abstract phenomenon; the people and situations in which we discover very concrete victims require a truly incarnate word to be worked out every time, with greater depth and commitment" (Navia 2004, 25).

In this sense, our proposal is focused on reflecting on the experience of Jesus and his family as immigrants experienced with the meaning of danger, flight, rootlessness, exile, and reinsertion in their own flesh. It is from this experience of exile by Jesus and his family that we want to briefly examine the complexity of the migration process—how it affects the family and how the family must adapt in order to overcome obstacles to survive. In such a concrete situation, such as that of Jesus and his family, who were forced to flee to Egypt in order to save their lives, we can see how this family, with the help of God, becomes a resilient family. In this sense, the theology of the resilient immigrant is centered on the experience of suffering:

rootlessness and exile, resilient reinsertion within crisis, accompaniment that promotes resilience.

Jesus and His Family Migrate into Exile (Suffering Experience)

> When they had left, an angel of the Lord appeared to Joseph in a dream and said to him, "Get up, take the child and his mother and flee to Egypt. Stay there until I call you, because Herod is going to look for the child to kill him." So he got up when it was still night, took the child and his mother, and left for Egypt, where he remained until the death of Herod. In this way was completed what the Lord had said through the prophet: "From Egypt I called my son." (Matt 2:13-15)

Matthew shows us an existing reality: migration to save one's life. This reality has been raised throughout this chapter: fleeing to save one's life, since in Honduras, as in many parts of Latin America, violence and criminality permeate society. During the period in which Jesus and his family fled to Egypt, many families or individuals migrated, some leaving their families behind, and Egypt was the ideal country to which Jews migrated, because of its proximity and because it offered more favorable options for survival, since there were Jewish settlements or colonies in the majority of Egyptian cities, which provided hospitality and support to new immigrants—often called transnational social networks or communities today.

The Capacity to Adapt (Resilient Reinsertion in a Crisis Situation)

When they reached Egypt, Joseph and Mary undoubtedly had to learn new ways of interacting with the surrounding culture and become accustomed to the food and at least some elements of the Egyptian languages—part of the process of adaptation upon migrating to another country. But such an undertaking generates crisis because it requires much time and effort and, above all, a supportive community of friends and relatives—the support of a social network.

Immigration implies an uprooting from sociocultural roots, causing confusion and displacement. The challenges of the language, food, and climate, among other things, produce a sense of insecurity and fear that turns into anxiety and pain. The decision to migrate is questioned, perhaps regretted. New physical challenges and emotional conflicts arise, even out of seemingly small issues, along with fatigue and changes in personality that coincide with culture shock (Radillo 2011, 147).

The Bible and exegetical studies do not specifically mention that Jesus and his family suffered these crises mentioned by Radillo, but it is likely that they had to be resilient in order to adapt to this new environment.

In closing, the theology of the resilient immigrant is a response to the suffering and pain experienced due to rootlessness, exile, and reinsertion that the family suffers in situations of migration. Resilience can be understood as "the capacity of human beings to face the adversities of life, overcome them and be transformed in a positive manner by them" (Munist et al. 1998).

This theology of the resilient immigrant is a theology that empties itself like company, memory, and prophecy; it is a narrative theology that constructs a new theological task from migrant pilgrim people who have experienced pain and suffering, exclusion, and rootlessness in a foreign country. From these realities of suffering legislation arises in favor of migrants, to receive them with love, respect, and solidarity.

Israel is a resilient people, from which resilient leaders and families historically arose with a great narrative of family, migration, and suffering. They offer important contributions to pastoral care in working from an immigrant pastoral perspective. From reading the Bible and from the resilient theology of the immigrant we seek answers in working with families who have endured the migration process. In this sense, we can start by reflecting on the following questions:

◈ Are there other families in the Bible who had to leave their birthplace? What were the reasons? Why do people migrate today? Discuss together the reasons for which the persons in the group migrated.

◈ What adjustments does an immigrant family have to make on an economical and emotional level? How does this affect the members of the family?

◈ How did Joseph, Mary, and Jesus experience the grace and care of God in exile and upon their return? How do we experience it today in the sense of belonging, encounter, identity, relationship?

✦ What can divorce and separation tell us about this new model of family life in which they find themselves? What are the advantages or disadvantages? How has it affected the life of the family and its dynamics?

Conclusion

In regard to the subject of forced migration due to slave economic models, together with the impact it has on the configuration and disconfiguration of new models of family life, many realities remain to be explored and analyzed, since migration and family are very complex subjects that deserve to be studied in more detail.

This chapter has emphasized the following points: Current economic models promote migration from our countries to the United States, and this is reflected in the pain and suffering that immigrants and their families are forced to experience during their journey while crossing several borders illegally. Compounding this fact are the psychosocial realities that women and their children must experience when they are abandoned and marginalized by fathers who have formed another family abroad. From those particular situations arise models of family life such as transnational families and blended families.

In some cases, there exists the ideal of reencounter or reunification, in which the illegal immigrant survives and helps the family he left behind; remittances and savings are used so that at a future time the family reunites and goes forward together. At this point we developed the theme of honor and shame.

It is shame that the woman suffers when she has to make the decision to rebuild her life in order to survive, but it is a positive shame, because she is empowered as a social actor who dignifies her life by leaving behind a sexist ideological subjection that has kept her in a state of oppression.

The issue of the legal character of the immigrant has been addressed in a biblical and theological manner, concluding that in the retrospective analysis of the memory of the people of God as a migrant people, laws that protect and care for the immigrant are apparent, and it is there where we develop the theory of a theology of the resilient immigrant as a basis for developing proposals of pastoral care from an immigrant pastoral perspective.

Bibliography

Baltodano, Mireya. "El espacio compartido." *Vida y pensamiento* 24, no. 1 (2004): 85–99.

Basch, L., N. Glick Schiller, and C. Blanc-Szanton, eds. "Towards a Transnational Perspective on Migration: Race, Class, Ethnicity, and Nationalism Reconsidered." *Annals of the New York Academy of Sciences*, vol. 645 (1992).

Brisson, Maryse. *Migraciones ¿alternativa insólita?* DEI: San José, 1997.

Duque, José. "¿Dónde acamparan los inmigrantes?" *Vida y pensamiento* 24, no. 1 (2004): 5–12.

Grosman, Cecilia, and Irene Martinez Alcorta. *Familias Ensambladas. Nuevas uniones después del divorcio. Ley y creencias. Problemas y soluciones legales.* Buenos Aires: Editorial Universidad, 2000, 9–10, 27–79.

Malina, Bruce. *Honor y Vergüenza: "Valores centrales del mundo mediterráneo del siglo primero" en el mundo del nuevo testamento. Perspectiva desde la antropología cultural.* Estella: Verbo Divino, 1995, 45–76.

Melillo, Aldo, and Elbio Néstor Suárez Ojeda, comps. *Resiliencia: Descubriendo las Propias Fortalezas.* Buenos Aires: Paidos, 2002, 83–122.

Navia, Carmiña. "El cuerpo de las mujeres y los hombres desplazados: notas para una llamada teológica. *Vida y pensamiento* 24, no. 1 (2004): 13–39.

Radillo, M. Rebeca. "El proceso migratorio: su impacto e implicaciones para la pastoral de la familiar en estados unidos." *Vida y pensamiento* 31, no. 1 (2011): 141–52.

Ramírez, José. "Inmigrantes en el antiguo testamento: realidad, problema y misterio." *Vida y pensamiento* 24, no. 1 (2004): 51–67.

Sánchez, R. "Cuando los hijos se quedan en el Salvador: modelos de incorporación, familias transnacionales y reunificación familiar." *Revista de Dialectología y Tradiciones Populares* 59, no. 2 (2004).

Tamez, Elsa. "Migración y desarraigo en la Biblia." *Vida y pensamiento* 24, no. 1 (2004): 69–84.

Vournien, P. "Family in Transition: Transnational Ties Identity Negotiation." *Proetnologia* 15 (2003).

CPSIA information can be obtained
at www.ICGtesting.com
Printed in the USA
BVHW030854080119
537203BV00035B/1467/P